The Journey Within

A Christian's Guide to

14 Non-traditional Spiritual Practices

Allison Brown, EdD

PUBLICATIONS, LLC

THE JOURNEY WITHIN:
A Christian's Guide to 14 Non-traditional Spiritual Practices

Copyright © 2021 by Allison Brown, EdD

Dr. Brown is represented by:

Tracy Crow
Tracy Crow Literary Agency, LLC
Phone: (727) 742-8346
Email: tracy@tracycrow.com

Published by:

Cactus Moon Publications, LLC;
info@cactusmoonpublishing.com
www.cactusmoonpublishing.com

ISBN: 978-1-7347865-2-1

Early Endorsements for The Journey Within

Truth has a resonance—essentially the same across all spiritual practices and wisdom tradition—Allison invites readers with a Christian perspective into this exploration that calls on trusting inner wisdom over outer rules and mindsets.

~Debra Moffitt, award-winning author of *Awake in the World,* and many others.

If you are looking to begin exploring new ways to manifest faith and connect with the Divine, The Journey Within is an essential starting point, and Allison Brown is an incredible guide.

~ Rev. Brandan J. Robertson, author of *Nomad: A Spirituality for Traveling Light* and Lead Pastor of Missiongathering Christian Church, San Diego, California

A must read for anyone seeking to uncover innate wisdom and a life of love and connection.

~ Dr. Jamie Turndorf, author of the #1 bestseller, *Love Never Dies: How to Reconnect and Make Peace with the Deceased,* and founder of AskDrLove.com

As souls continue to awaken in search of their own truth, they will seek guidance toward their spiritual path while still honoring their religious beliefs. When that happens, they will reach for this book.

> ~ Rena Huisman, Psychic Medium, and author of *The Would-Be Medium: My Ten-Year Journey as a Workshop Junkie*

Bravo to Dr. Brown for having the courage to show her fellow Christians that rather than being off-limits, the practices she demystifies here hold great potential for their soul's growth.

> ~ Suzanne Giesemann, CDR, USN (Ret.), author of *Messages of Hope* and many others

The Journey Within is dedicated to my children,
Evan and Natalie.
You are loved beyond words!
Go boldly into this world, honoring your Truth.

Acknowledgments

First and foremost, I am eternally grateful to my husband and soul mate, William, who honored his internal knowing—that I was THE ONE—and who predicted, 30 years ago, that this book was coming. Someone once said that behind every great man is a great woman, but the opposite is also true. My accomplishments would not have been possible without your support. I love you!

Thank you, Jeanne Brown, for raising and nurturing this amazing man and for loving me like your own daughter.

A heartfelt thank you to my dad, Sam—your unconditional love and unending support gave me the confidence to succeed.

I am grateful for the friends and family members who provided not only encouragement but valuable editorial feedback, especially Brenda Brown, Judy Buchanan, LeeAnn Carroll, Debra Ceasario, Donna Jenkins, Donna Kennedy, and Cindy Blazer Lawrence.

Thank you, Debra Moffitt for your inspiration, guidance, and faith in my ability. You got this ball rolling.

A huge shout out to Neale Donald Walsch for your kind words and valuable advice, provided without a trace of expectation. I was tickled pink by that divinely orchestrated encounter!

Many, many thanks to my generous endorsers: Candace Craw-Goldman, Suzanne Giesemann, Rena Huisman, Priscilla Keresey, Brandan Robertson, and Jamie Turndorf. That you took the time to read and review the work of an "unknown," previously-unpublished author is humbling. Your words mean more than you know.

I am grateful for fellow military veteran, Dr. Kate Hendricks Thomas, whose passionate research has enabled veterans to heal through the integration of personal spiritual practices such as those described in this book.

Thank you, Lisa Pane, for your expertise. You made the editing process quite easy.

I am grateful for my amazing agent Tracy Crow, who works with me not just from her head but from her heart. And that's a big deal. Thank you for *knowing*.

I owe a debt of gratitude to Lily Gianna Woodmansee at Cactus Moon Publications who took a chance on a first-time author. Your *yes* helped make this dream a reality!

Thank you, as well, to the entire Cactus Moon team who worked diligently behind the scenes on my behalf.

Last but certainly not least, I am immeasurably grateful for my guides and helpers across the veil who remind me daily that I am loved, I am supported, and I am eternal.

Foreword

There's nothing angry or judgmental about God—though many of us were led to believe this. That mindset reaches far back into antiquity where religious teachers imposed harsh beliefs to instill fear in spiritual seekers and take power over us. That old paradigm led to rigid belief systems that continue to incite fear and doesn't serve those who yearn to expand and grow.

Jesus was a rebel. He didn't fit into the paradigm of the time and, by many of today's standards, he wouldn't fit in a traditional Christian church. His acts of healing people through touch; apparently defying the laws of physics (or working with them on the quantum level) by creating fish and bread and turning water to wine would be considered witchcraft. His greatest miracle—the one that endures over 2,000 years later—is the pure, unconditional love of all including those who were ill, poor, prostitutes, and even taxmen. This love continues to be the heart of his legacy.

The texts about him emerged years after his ascension. His story found its way into the Bible after much political wrangling about how to present it, and many different interpretations and translations of the texts carried deep biases. These became the foundations of today's current Christian religion. In her book, *The Journey Within*, Allison shares about her inner call to grow, her questioning of that tradition, and how she broke free of the rigid mindset established over the centuries. By confronting her feelings that there had to be more, and asking good questions, her life expanded. This resonates with me. I grew up in a fundamentalist Christian environment and grappled with many of the same questions. Allison invites readers with a Christian perspective into an exploration that calls on trusting inner wisdom over outer rules and mindsets, and she presents the background of different tools like yoga, meditation, astrology and Reiki to demystify them.

Truth has a resonance, and it is essentially the same across all spiritual practices and wisdom traditions. You'll know its presence by asking a few simple questions: 1) Is it non-violent? 2) Does it express compassion? 3) Does it encourage questioning and self-inquiry over following outer codes and rules? 4) Is it benevolent? And 5) Does it foster respect and love of self and others? As you read Allison's story and explore the fourteen practices presented here, I encourage you to listen to that deeper inner voice of your intuition for what resonates with you.

As you explore the practices, I invite you to give yourself permission to become aware of the rigid mindsets and beliefs that no longer serve you. Let go of them and allow any sense of guilt and of feelings that you could be betraying Jesus to dissolve. Remember the example of Jesus, the rebel, who showed the way by breaking with set traditions and walking a unique path of love. Allow for the possibility that your wise self knows the way for you. Asking from within, give space to exploring with curiosity and set out on adventure of discovery. Be bold and courageous, knowing that you're being called by love and your soul's yearning for expansion and more and more love.

My wish for you as you read is that you move at least a little out of your comfort zone. It's part of the exploration process. You may find that your spiritual life will gain more depth and your self-confidence will grow as you learn to trust the guidance of your inner wisdom. Your discernment to choose what is ideal for you becomes a part of the process, so take what works and speaks to you and leave the rest. As you work the puzzle of what's right for you, you may also begin to rediscover your own gifts of healing, intuitive insight, creativity and more. These will empower you to step into a whole new place of expanded awareness guided by wise self-direction. The path leads to feeling more and more love, contentment, Self-confidence, freedom, peace and joy as life unfolds.

With Love and Gratitude,
Debra Moffitt

Debra Moffitt is the Award-winning Author of *Awake in the World* and many others.

Author's Note

October 19, 2020

I've always believed that everything happens in divine timing, and this book project is no exception. Everything about this book—its conception, the writing process, finding an agent, and securing a publisher—has been beautifully and perfectly orchestrated. Therefore, I wasn't terribly surprised when, over the weekend, my publisher suggested to my agent that we speed up the publication date a bit.

Given the year we've had that's included a global pandemic and lockdowns, I'd have to agree that the timing certainly feels right. As I sit down to pen this note, the events of this year weigh heavily on my mind. I liken it to a giant snow globe—humanity is being shaken out of complacency, our very foundation crumbling beneath us. The territory we've been navigating is foreign—there is no map, no playbook, and sometimes, not even a handrail. It's as if we are being collectively propelled (often, against our wishes) by some invisible force, into a new way of being, a new way of existing. One could say we are journeying *together* into a new and unfamiliar world. A world that we will create—intentionally or unintentionally—*together*.

Many would call this a time of crisis. In fact, it might be more aptly described as a series of crises, one after another, like a giant tetherball knocking us down again and again on each pass. But a crisis—as painful as it often is—can also usher in a turning point, a divinely-guided intersection with life. Collectively, it is during times of crisis that human beings discover previously untapped sources of compassion, courage, and love. Individually, a dark night of the soul, often leads to a deeper sense of purpose once we've given ourselves time to reflect and heal.

It is my hope that the tools presented in this book will assist you, as they have assisted me, in using this time of chaos as an opportunity for growth. Throughout the long, challenging months of 2020, I've found that these practices help me access deeper reserves of compassion and forgiveness, recognize truth in all forms, and embody unity consciousness. My morning yoga practice keeps me mentally and physically flexible, while Reiki works to keep anxiety at bay. Meditation has also been invaluable, allowing me the time and space to address patterns, habits, or belief systems that do not serve my highest good. And these are but a few examples of the tools in action.

I have no way to know where we will be on our collective journey at the time this book is released. Perhaps we will see a glimmer of light at the end of the tunnel. What I know for sure, however, is that our collective "recovery" must begin individually, within each and every one of us. It is only from this place of internal peace that we will create a peaceful, new world. It can be no other way.

To that end, as we navigate this unpredictable, external journey, let us simultaneously embark on a parallel journey…the journey within.

Table of Contents

Chapter 1 - Why this Book? 1

Chapter 2 - What About the Bible? 17

Part One: Self-Discovery 37

Chapter 3 - Meditation 49

Chapter 4 - Moving Meditation: Qigong and Tai Chi...... 57

Chapter 5 - Yoga.. 65

Chapter 6 - Reincarnation and Past Life Exploration 71

Chapter 7 - Astrology 81

Resources: Part One 91

Part Two: Communication 93

Chapter 8 - Numerology 107

Chapter 9 - Tarot and Oracle Cards 117

Chapter 10 - Psychics and Mediums........................ 125

Chapter 11 - Angels 133

Resources: Part Two... 145

Part Three: Healing.. 147

Chapter 12 - Acupuncture and Acupressure................ 163

Chapter 13 - Craniosacral Therapy 169

Chapter 14 - Reiki... 175

Chapter 15 - Tapping Therapy 183

Chapter 16 - Crystals and Healing Stones........................191

Chapter 17 - Your Journey Awaits 203

Resources: Part Three 209

"Until you make the unconscious conscious, it will direct your life and you will call it fate."
Carl Jung

Chapter 1 - Why this Book?

Congratulations! Something led you to pick up this book, and I thank you for honoring that impulse. What you are holding is a *spiritual reference guide* for seekers, particularly Christian seekers like me, who are looking for something that can't be satisfied by mainstream religion. Perhaps, like me, you were raised in a conservative Christian household but had this nagging feeling that the things you were taught just didn't add up, didn't quite jive with your inner *knowingness*. Maybe you are a practicing Christian with an open mind and simply want to investigate what's out there. Some of you may feel uncomfortable with your church's stance on divorce, homosexuality, birth control, or life after death. Others of you may simply be searching for a comprehensive guide to some of the most common non-traditional spiritual practices, along with an explanation of their historical underpinnings. Whatever the motivation, you selected this book for a reason. Your heart is seeking answers—a reconciliation, of sorts—between your modern-day experiences and your traditional Christian upbringing. It is my sincere desire that you will find some of those answers in this book. At the very least, I hope that you will read with an open mind and come to your own conclusions—decide for yourself what you believe about the topics presented.

Each day people all across the world are waking up to the realization that they are more than just a physical body on the treadmill of life, that living is more than chasing a paycheck and crossing tasks off our ever-growing to-do lists. More and more people are acknowledging that humans are, first and foremost, spiritual beings with an *instinctual* desire to connect to something greater than ourselves. We believe there is a greater purpose to our lives, and in order to lead a fulfilling life, we must find and act on that purpose. These ideas, urgings, and sense of restlessness used to be symptomatic of the so-called midlife crisis, but in reality, it's happening more frequently and to men and women of all ages.

New Age Movement

This collective search for meaning began in earnest in the early 1970s and was dubbed the New Age movement, a bit of a misnomer, considering that most of those New Age concepts actually stemmed from ancient traditions. The 1960s counterculture decade provided the context in which this line of thinking could flourish, but fairly quickly, the ideas started to take hold in the mainstream. They were no longer the sole possession of the hippies. Fifty years later, this movement has led to a worldwide, collective transformation that many believe will guide us into a new way of being—a world in which all inhabitants understand their individual and collective purpose and use that purpose for the good of all humankind. This universal movement seeks to create a world of harmony, love, enlightenment and true progress.

Throughout history people have sought to quench their thirst for meaning through organized religion. After all, isn't that the purpose of religion? Some religions, in fact, claim to be the ONLY path to God. A good number of people, however, have found that many of the ideas espoused by organized religion no longer resonate, and they have started to look for answers in other places. These so-called *New Agers* still seek a spiritual experience, but they prefer a *direct* spiritual experience rather than one that comes couched in a religious framework or relies on a human intermediary. They believe that *eternal truth* is contained within each one of us. Therefore, they are more concerned with *finding these truths* than with the actual *path* of discovery, as it is considered a uniquely individual process.

The evidence that people are no longer satisfied with the answers they find in mainstream religion is born out in the data. Research has shown that only twenty-seven percent of millennials attend a weekly religious service. According to Duval's church-attendance statistics, although forty percent of people *say* they attend a weekly religious service, according to the statistics less than twenty percent actually do. And between 2007 and 2014, although the U.S. population increased by sixteen million, church attendance declined by 3.7 percent. Shattuck's data predicts that by 2050, church attendance will have dropped to almost half of what it was in 1990.

To address their declining attendance, the mainstream church tries to appeal to the young or disillusioned by creating charismatic, non-denominational mega-churches, replete with live bands and coffee bars. Unfortunately, the underlying message hasn't changed. Although church attendance often satisfies the need for social interaction, rarely does it help us transcend to an enlightened, more Christ-like state of being. Many believe that this decline signals a transformation in how we understand and experience God. It is no longer just the New Agers who find it increasingly difficult to embrace the distant God of conventional religion. On the contrary, God can be found everywhere and is, therefore, accessible to all. With that in mind, many Christians find themselves on a journey to locate this personal, relevant God.

Why I am Telling You This

To understand my rationale for writing a spiritual reference book for Christians, let me share a little bit about my own background. My brother and I grew up in a typical household in Wilmington, North Carolina, with two parents and a dog. We were brought up in the ultra-stoic Episcopal Church, and we immersed ourselves in church activities. We attended advent and Christmas church services, replete with the pageant, carols and scripture readings that detailed the birth of Jesus. On Christmas Eve, the family would get dressed up and attend the candlelight service, where we would sing my favorite Christmas carols (oh, how I love Christmas carols!). After the service, we came home, and my brother and I were allowed to open one gift from under the tree. On Easter, there were always brand new outfits, Easter lilies, photo ops, along with the story of Jesus's death and resurrection. Occasionally, we would get up early for the sunrise service after which the church would provide a delicious breakfast. My brother and I attended teenage lock-ins and youth trips, and we faithfully took our communion class and became acolytes—assistants to the priest.

As my brother and I grew older, our family became one of *those* families—the ones who came only for the big services—Easter and Christmas. By then, my mother had become more of a holy roller, immersed in studying her Bible and watching Pat Robertson's 700 Club on the television, and my dad was finding her ever more difficult to relate to. Eventually, they divorced after my first year of college, leaving her to seek solace in her new church family, the kind of people who sang robustly, flailed their hands wildly, and shouted praises during the service. As one would expect from a *true believer*, my mother, who had been a stay-at-home mom all those years, refused to stand up for herself during the divorce, insisting that to do so would mean that she agreed with it. Sadly, she never did regain her footing, taking menial part-time jobs when necessary, and eventually moving back in with her mother, my grandmother, until her death at fifty-nine.

Once or twice, I attended church with her. Although I was uncomfortable, simply because as a burgeoning adult, I did not yet know who I was and was uncomfortable with a lot of things, I respected the fact that these people could *celebrate* their faith. They could let loose, sing and be *joyful* about what they believed, unlike in the mainstream church, where being a quiet, non-questioning member of the flock was the expectation. Either way, the message I kept hearing within the Christian church, no matter the denomination, was that there was only one path to Heaven—*theirs*. They interpreted Jesus's message to be exclusive rather than inclusive. I heard about my sinful nature and the perils of hell. Humans were blessed with free will, they said, but if we chose incorrectly, we would suffer eternal damnation. I remember thinking, even as a child, that it just didn't add up.

Around thirteen, sincerely curious about the inconsistencies in my faith, I questioned my priest during a summer camp. I asked about the kind of God who would allow almost seventy percent of His own creation to perish just because they either were not Christians or were in some remote location where they weren't *lucky* enough to have heard the Christian message. I'm pretty sure I didn't ask the question quite so boldly; nevertheless, although I don't recall his exact response, it was evident that he was displeased and that I should never venture into that topic of conversation again.

As an adult, having converted to a Methodist church, I asked again. This time it was during a Christian woman's conference, and I questioned the female youth pastor of our church, who was a friend. Her response was what was to be expected from an indoctrinated clergy member—something about the fact that, since we are sinners at birth, no one on their own would get into heaven anyway, but because Jesus came to Earth and then died for us, as atonement for our sins, we (Christians) are saved and will enter through the Pearly Gates. Therefore, as they see it, it isn't a matter of excluding others, it is a matter of *including* Christians—those who believe that Jesus died for the sins of mankind. Again this just didn't resonate with my inner *knowingness*.

In spite of my constant misgivings, I stuck with the Christian Church, too afraid to give up everything and everyone in order to live my Truth. After all, I believed in Jesus and his message of love, and I didn't want to throw the baby out with the bath water (pun intended). Besides, my new Methodist church family was an awesome group of people! By then, I had married, moved to Texas, and given birth to two children one year apart. My husband, Bill, and I bonded with the pastor, and our church was instrumental in the success of our marriage and the raising of our young children. It was during this time that I first *heard* God (the Holy Spirit) speaking to me. I was being led to create a hands-on healing team at my church. I can't explain how I knew—I just knew. (Today, I would recognize this as a form of *claircognizance* – knowing something to be true without any logical explanation.) Suffice it to say I knew that I was being prompted by a force outside myself to do something that was completely out of my comfort zone. There was no question that I had to follow through, even though I had never had an experience like that before.

Our church had a new pastor by then, and my family had a good relationship with him, as well. I made an appointment to speak with him, although I did not tell him on the phone what I had in mind. As soon as I sat down in his office and shared my plan, he informed me that he had received a message (presumably from the same God), that someone would be coming to see him about this very thing. I had no reason to doubt his word. (And today, given what I know now, I am even more certain he was telling the truth.) The pastor's words excited me beyond belief! I wasn't crazy. God really was speaking to me, using me to serve others. I had often prayed to be a servant, to be used for the greater good of the Universe, and here was the answer to my prayer.

The creation of the healing team was a critical turning point for me for two reasons. Most importantly, it was the first time I recall receiving a clear message from Spirit. It was my first big A-HA moment! I *did* have a job to do here on Earth, and this was my first assignment. Second, although I wouldn't understand this until much later, it was the first acknowledgment of my role as a healer. I had been called to serve others through the gift of healing. Around this same time, I found and read Neale Donald Walsch's first book, *Conversations with God*. This book was another turning point in my life because it completely affirmed what I had been feeling all those years. I devoured all of the books in the series, as well as Neale's other works. Although the books resonated with me and finally gave me a framework for my own belief system, it made me feel like a fraud around my friends and within my congregation. Little by little, however, I was able to make decisions that reflected my Truth, rather than the truth of the mainstream Christian Church.

Bill and the kids and I moved to South Carolina, and we found another Methodist church where I was able to do some hands-on healing, although not in a team format. We attended for a few years and I continued to wrestle with myself. Eventually, however, we moved to a neighboring town where we built a house and searched, unsuccessfully, for a church closer to our new home. None of the churches we tried ever felt like the family we had left behind in Texas. Even though I didn't believe in the teachings of the church, our Texas church family had been a close-knit, loving support system for our growing family, and we made some wonderful friends who we still keep in contact with. I don't know that I would have survived with two babies, twelve months and two weeks apart, were it not for some of those friends. For the next nine years, however, we were churchless.

During this time, as I was figuring out my place within the general spiritual community, I kept hearing about a healing modality called Reiki. In fact, one of my college students (at the time, I taught online Education courses for a major university in addition to being a school counselor) offhandedly mentioned in one of her emails to me that she was a Reiki Master. I think we had been discussing strategies for stress reduction in children, which led to a conversation about stress-reduction techniques in general. Sometime after the course had ended, curiosity getting the best of me, I corresponded with her about the topic of Reiki. It seemed like a way to complement my healing practice or perhaps to provide a *formal* protocol in which to work. She agreed to send me a long-distance Reiki session. Although I didn't feel any noticeable difference, based on what I know today, I believe the energy was working on me at a spiritual level, preparing me for what was to come.

Even after that experience, it still took me a couple of years to be drawn toward Reiki training because my upbringing had scared me away from anything that even *remotely* conflicted with mainstream Christianity. This included practices like yoga and acupuncture, but especially anything that involved communicating with the Spirit realm, like the Ouija Board, tarot cards, mediums and psychics. Eventually I grew tired of being afraid. I wanted to feel empowered, confident and courageous, able to explore my Truth from a place of love rather than fear. One day while scanning my Facebook account, a post caught my eye about a Reiki I class being taught in my area. I contacted the instructor, and the rest is history! (I have since become a Reiki Master Teacher myself). That was another huge leap out of my comfort zone and led to a yearlong exploration of many of these esoteric, metaphysical, New Age topics. Along the way, I was forced, once and for all, to reconcile my newfound beliefs with my traditional Christian upbringing. Luckily, I found that they are not mutually exclusive.

As I explored these previously taboo topics, I had to learn to rely on my internal compass to determine what rang true and resonated with my soul. This was difficult because my Christian upbringing had taught me to depend on other people—clergy members, parents, and other faith leaders—for guidance. Of course, the Bible serves as the ultimate Christian rule book, but let's face it, some of it can be confusing or contradictory. There-fore, we often look to the *experts* for interpretation. For me, it was a challenging predicament—going within (meditation) wasn't permitted but searching outside of myself could lead me astray. For example, how could I tell if I were truly communi-cating with Jesus (the Holy Spirit) or with Satan in disguise? My religious leaders would have said that if, after praying, the mes-sage seemed to conflict with the literal interpretation of the Bible (or their own interpretation), it was not of God. But that seemed like circular reasoning to me: 1) Read the Bible and pray for meaning. 2) If the message you receive contradicts your leader's interpretation of the Bible, it must be wrong. 3) Go back to #1. Wait, what? This type of dilemma tends to force well-meaning Christians to abdicate their own authority and look to others for answers. As I practiced, however, I got better at hearing my own internal voice, that inner *knowingness* that had been nudging me all along.

Throughout my exploration I found myself wondering what it was about each of these topics that had Christians up in arms. What were they so afraid of? Many of the things I studied, in fact, appeared quite compatible with Christian doctrine once I got past some of the vocabulary. For instance, although the words *Reiki* and *energy healing* initially set off my Christian alarm bell, I found that I was utilizing the same healing touch—the same loving energy—that I used as a member of my church's healing team. The energy emanating from my hands came from the same source. Another example surrounds meditation. Although some Christians are fearful of the practice of meditation, when you dig a little deeper it really serves the same purpose as the Christian practice of contemplation. Contemplation describes the *experiential* knowledge of God (the Source of All), an opening of the heart and the mind—the same thing that the meditator is seeking.

New Thought Movement

During my research I found that beginning in the mid-nineteenth century a New Thought movement arose, perhaps in an attempt to answer some of the very same questions I had been asking. Many of the New Thought proponents were Christians who sought to follow Jesus's teachings, some of which they believed had been hijacked and misrepresented by early (and subsequent) church leaders to fit their own agendas. Today, although there are several New Thought organizations in existence, such as Unity Worldwide Ministries and Agape International Spiritual Center, their foundational values are almost identical. Among their core beliefs are the sacredness of all of creation, the interconnectedness and interdependence of all life, and the creative nature of human consciousness, manifested through our thoughts and feelings.

The Rev. Tom Thorpe, an ordained Unity minister who also serves as a faculty member and subject matter expert at Unity Institute and Seminary's Spiritual Education and Enrichment program, calls himself a Metaphysical Christian, another name for a Christian who follows the New Thought philosophy. He believes that the gateway to all Truth can be found through the unencumbered study of Jesus's teachings. Rev. Thorpe contends that everyone (Christians included) has not only the right, but the responsibility to discover his/her own Truth based on a personal practice of study, reflection, and experience. Unfortunately, many Christians (like me) carry around the excess baggage of negative religious experiences, clouding their ability to see or even search for this Truth.

Although the New Age movement was birthed from this New Thought philosophy, it is sometimes considered nothing more than a collection of non-traditional spiritual practices unable to be neatly wrapped into any single religious *package*. These practices, therefore, need to be unwrapped and individually inspected to determine whether they are relevant or helpful as we seek to connect with God. Rather than cavalierly discarding anything with a New Age label, perhaps it would be beneficial to investigate some of these concepts and decide for ourselves which are of value, which ones resonate with our own *inner knowingness*. In so doing, we give ourselves permission, as Rev. Thorpe described, to study, reflect on and experience for ourselves some non-traditional spiritual practices that may very well illuminate our path.

The spiritual practices described in this book spring from a few core New Age beliefs, three of which provide the foundation for this book: 1) A belief in the spiritual authority of the Self, 2) a belief in the idea that human beings can communicate with a wide variety of non-human (non-physical) entities or spiritual beings, and 3) a belief in alternative healing modalities, particularly those that draw on universal life energy. This resource guide, therefore, organizes the various topics and practices into those same three areas: self-discovery, communication, and healing. Each of the three sections begins with the philosophical and historical background of the belief system that grounds the practices within that section. The chapters within each section provide a description of some of the most common practices within that belief system.

This book is the resource that I wished I'd had as I explored these so-called taboo topics, searching for the answers to two questions: *What is this all about? What makes it taboo?* While not exhaustive, this resource covers some of the most common, non-traditional, spiritual practices a Christian seeker might run across. I consider it to be an exploratory tool since all of these topics have entire books (or hundreds of books) written about them. This book is designed to provide an overview of topics that Christians, or anyone, might wish to explore further.

Chapter 2 - What About the Bible?

One of the roadblocks I encountered as a Christian seeker was that the Bible was, almost always, the sole source of "evidence" against many of the ideas I wanted to investigate. A short search on Amazon will easily uncover volumes of material, written by educated, well-meaning folks, that disparage the spiritual practices found in this book and are meant to admonish any New Age apologists, particularly Christians (like me). For the most part, these authors use the Bible as their rationale for debunking these practices, and actually, that is a sensible Christian approach. Anyone even remotely familiar with the Bible could probably pluck out a good number of verses that would bolster their argument. The Bible, after all, is considered by most (if not all) Christians to be the *inspired* Word of God. It serves as the ultimate Christian *rule book*.

The thing about inspiration is that it is naturally filtered through the one-who-is-inspired. Consider for a moment a majestic sculpture, a beautiful symphony, or a touching poem. Artistic works like these are often said to have been inspired. Without a doubt they are inspirational to those who see, hear, or read them. But the message that the artist sensed during the creation process and intended to convey could very well differ from the message that is received by the viewer, listener, or reader. For example, I'm an avid reader and have participated in a number of book clubs. Rarely have we all agreed on the author's meaning or intent with regard to a particular passage, plot twist, or ending. Heck, I remember one instance when two members had such completely different assumptions from the outset that it altered their perspective on the entire book! This struggle is even more pronounced when reading poetry. Poems have the ability to evoke any number of diverse feelings and emotions, depending upon the reader's background, emotional state, culture, or familiarity with the author. I can still hear my son complaining about his English Literature class in high school. An exam question asked about the meaning of a particular line of poetry, and his answer had been marked wrong. "But mom, how does the teacher know what the author meant?" Now, I'm sure the *correct* answer had been discussed in class, but his complaint still serves to illustrate my point about works of art.

As I began to explore my spirituality, I realized that unless I wanted to keep living in the closet, I eventually had to come out with my Truth. This meant that I had to do some research. I needed to reconcile the knowledge in my head with the feelings in my heart. On one hand, I understood all of the rules and rituals of Christianity. After all, I'm a good student—a teacher's pet, even. On the other hand, my heart was calling me to something bigger. I felt compelled to seek out my Truth...to step out of my comfort zone in order to experience a relationship with God that was beyond the boundaries of my neat little Christian box. I was being drawn toward a relationship that came from the heart, not the head. What I found was that in order to dispel the fear I had acquired and fully commit to what was blooming in my heart, I had to be able to rationalize the things in my head. I needed to figure out why there was such a discrepancy between the *truth* I had been taught and the Truth I sensed on the inside. With that in mind, I'd like to share some of my research, saving you the time it would take to explore these issues yourself.

When we consider the Bible, viewing it as an inspired Work, there are a few issues we must first examine, because as we have just established, quite a few things can influence our perspective. For starters, we should address the fact that some folks take the Bible literally—they read the Bible as one would read a history textbook, for example (about thirty percent of Americans, according to David Lose, president of The Lutheran Theological Seminary of Philadelphia). Folks in the second camp believe that the Bible is subject to interpretation, that it was not meant to be taken literally. Before we wade too deeply into the issue of Bible interpretation, let's take a look at the first camp – those who believe that the Bible, because it is considered the infallible Word of God, should be read in its literal form.

Literal Bible Interpretation

David Lose, in addition to his role at The Lutheran Theolog-ical Seminary, is the author of several books, including *Making*

Sense of Scripture: Big Questions about the Book of Faith. He is considered an authority on Bible reading, as he routinely crisscrosses the country, teaching people of faith how to read scripture with confidence and enjoyment. Lose provides several convincing reasons not to take the Bible literally.

But the Bible itself never claims to be factually accurate. Many "literalists," he says, support their claim of the Bible's inerrancy with 2 Timothy 3:16: "All scripture is inspired by God and is useful for teaching, for reproof, for correction, and for training in righteousness." As Lose explains, being *inspired* by God is not the same thing as being *factually accurate*. The various authors of the Bible probably never imagined that their accounts would one day be subject to fact-checking. On the contrary, the purpose of their testimony was an attempt to persuade or witness to others that they might come to understand the nature of Love as modeled by Jesus. If the biblical authors wrote to profess their faith, rather than to record an accurate account of historical events, it is then easier to reconcile the frequent discrepancies that sometimes create doubt about its trustworthiness. Lose suggests that instead of wondering which Gospel author *got it right*, we should seek to understand the significance behind their various perspectives.

A second reason that Lose believes the Bible should not be read literally is revealed in the nature of the Bible's main characters, many of whom had serious flaws. Cain and Moses were murderers; David was a murderer *and* an adulterer; Jacob was a liar; Noah got drunk; and Peter denied Jesus, not once, but three times. In other words, they were imperfect human beings. As any Christian knows, God regularly chooses ordinary people to accomplish extraordinary tasks, including the creation of what could arguably be considered the most influential book in the world. A literalist approach to Bible reading overlooks the fact that the Bible was written by these same, fallible individuals. Lose explains that, whether intentional or not, the literalist's perspective requires the Bible to be both fully human and fully Divine, a characteristic that is normally attributed only to Jesus.

A final reason that Lose says Christians should not rely on a literal reading of the Bible is that it has not been common practice throughout history. In fact, the doctrine surrounding the Bible's *inerrancy*, upheld by literalists, has only come about in the past 150 years. For example, St. Augustine, the renowned Christian theologian, was at first turned off to Christianity in part because of his disdain for Old Testament scripture. He took issue with the literal interpretation of Bible stories, such as Jonah and the whale. It was only after Ambrose, bishop of Milan, taught him the meaning of allegorical interpretation—whereby scripture could be examined for spiritual truths rather than historical facts—that he was able to take the Bible seriously.

Christians as far back as Saint Ambrose understood that the Bible is made up of a variety of literary styles, including Historical Narrative (Acts), Prophecy (Revelation), Biography (Luke), Parables (used primarily by Jesus in the Gospels), Poetry (Psalms), Epistle/Letter (2 Timothy), and Statutory/Law (Genesis). Within those various styles, the writers also use a number of literary devices, such as similes, metaphors, imagery, symbolism, and irony, to communicate their message. Interpreting the Bible literally, without regard for literary devices, would then mean that Solomon's bride really did have doves in place of her eyes (Song of Solomon 4:1) and humans are little more than lumps of clay (Isaiah 64:8)—unless, of course, we selectively determine which passages are subject to a literal translation and which are not.

David Lose, in my mind, beautifully illustrates one of the most common dilemmas we Christians wrestle with—which is whether to take the Bible literally or not. I think most Christians, like me, want to take parts of the Bible literally, but also realize (like St. Augustine) that some things simply sound too farfetched to be taken at face value. For example, my intelligent mind understood that the Earth probably wasn't created in six days; most likely, a *day* simply represented some other length of time. On the other hand, I truly believed that we would one day find Noah's Ark. In other words, I tended to pick and choose which parts I believed were factually accurate and which were not. But any lawyer worth his salt understands that in order to effectively argue our case, we must be consistent in our application of principle. This is why I was torn.

Non-literal Bible Interpretation

So, how *do* we interpret the Bible if we can't take it literally? Some folks believe we should simply apply common or *plain* sense when reading the Bible. In other words, we should take the passages at face value. *Plain sense* Bible reading is similar to a literal interpretation, in that we don't try to *read into* the scripture, but it does allow for the use of literary devices, because we are reading within the context of our own twenty-first century background. Although this sounds reasonable, there are a couple of problems with this approach.

The first issue with a plain sense reading of the Bible is the very fact that we are applying a twenty-first century frame of reference to a book written by people with a vastly different perspective of the world. What makes sense to us today, given our current cultural, religious and social context, may not bear any resemblance to what the Bible's authors had in mind. For example, the commandment "Thou shalt not kill," interpreted within today's context, often refers only to premeditated murder—many Christians are not at odds with killing another human being within the context of capital punishment, self-defense, or war. Did God, when he gave the Ten Commandments to Moses intend for modern human beings to apply these caveats?

Another problem with applying our own common sense when reading the Bible is that even within a twenty-first century perspective, each reader will naturally filter the text through his/her own background—knowledge of—scripture, emotional state, cultural framework, age, education, or any number of unique characteristics. A Millennial has a completely different frame of reference, for example, than a Baby Boomer. A Christian raised in the United States may interpret a scripture much differently than a Christian raised in Botswana. To make matters worse, even Christians from the same geographical region don't agree on certain aspects of Bible interpretation. This is evident in the dizzying array of Christian denominations and practices. As a Methodist, for example, I drank grape juice during communion, but my Episcopalian church served wine to both children and adults. Infant baptism is not practiced in all denominations, and when it isn't, the reasons vary. Catholics condemn birth control; Orthodox Christians routinely fast; Southern Baptists prohibit the ordination of women; and Assemblies of God members eschew dancing. If religious leaders heading up the various Christian denominations don't agree, how can we expect the layperson to get it right?

Many Bible scholars do agree with certain tried-and-true methods related to Bible interpretation. First of all, because the books were written by different people, in order to best understand the message, we must reflect upon the author's purpose and audience. What was s/he trying to say and to whom was s/he speaking? As an educator, I speak to all kinds of audiences, from young students to parents and fellow staff members. Even within the same broad topic my content and delivery will vary tremendously depending on my audience. If a parent read the transcript of a talk I gave to students, for example, the message would probably seem unclear—they might be confused or have questions.

After getting clear about the author's purpose and audience, we must next take into consideration the general context of the passage as well as the historical context in which it was written. It is not wise to isolate and interpret an individual passage out of context. This one seems like a no-brainer, right? After all, we've probably all been quoted out of context at some point in our lives. Little children, when learning to read, are encouraged to *consider the context* when deciphering a word's meaning. With regard to the Bible, though, we must also consider the *historical* context. Now, I don't know about you, but history is not my strength. As a Christian, in order for me to be completely clear on certain passages of scripture, I had to consult a reference book or rely on my priest or pastor. For me, neither of those options was ideal. Luckily, I found a third option.

The most important recommendation of a number of Christian leaders, including the Rev. Roger Wolsey, an author and ordained United Methodist pastor who directs the Wesley Foundation at the University of Colorado at Boulder, is that we *prayerfully* seek to understand the Bible, calling upon the Holy Spirit to help us discern the meaning and message. We must read and examine God's Word for ourselves, rather than placing our trust in others. As Paul said, "The natural man receiveth not the things of the Spirit of God: for they are foolishness unto him: neither can he know them, because they are spiritually discerned." (1 Cor. 2:14). The Bible does not advise us to blindly follow our religious leaders or to dodge the tough questions. God seems to suggest that we use our minds—the minds that He created within us—to study His Word carefully. Paul commended the people of Berea because "they received the word with all readiness of mind and searched the scriptures daily to see if these things were so." (Acts 17:11).

This advice challenges us to seek a more personal, intimate interpretation of scripture with the same fervor that we pursue an experiential knowledge of and relationship with God Himself. Then, through our own study, reflection, and experience, we will receive "the spirit which is of God; that we might know the things that are freely given to us of God." (1 Cor. 2:12). As Rev. Thorpe explains, the Bible is not a textbook that tells us what we must believe. Rather, it invites us to explore the hearts and minds of Jesus's early followers, the founders of our Judeo-Christian tradition. When we study scripture from a metaphysical framework, we are able to build our own understanding using their insights and experiences.

This explanation made perfect sense to me. It allowed me to follow my heart, using the Bible as a way to *explore* the new ideas I encountered. Not only was I freed from having to rely on the interpretation of others, I was being led to take responsibility for my own learning. In fact, Rev. Wolsey implores us *not* to place our spiritual development into the hands of others. Instead of abdicating my authority, I was being challenged to *trust* my own internal compass to guide my interpretation of scripture.

But wait! Even though I was being given a green light to prayerfully explore my Bible, I quickly realized that I had quite a few Bibles, all of which were written in a different style. Some, such as the King James Version, were formal and were often used during our church service. Others were more conversational and were typically used during Bible studies to enhance our understanding of scripture. Which one was best? What I found through further research was that, in addition to contemplating Bible interpretation, we must also consider Bible translation. The same scripture read from two different translations could potentially lead the reader to two very different conclusions. The more I learned, the more I realized how important it would be to hone my internal compass. That way, no matter which Bible I read, I could rely on the meaning that resonated with my inner being. Rather than trying to use my head, I could "listen" with my heart.

Bible Translation

Our examination of the Bible as an inspirational Work would be incomplete without a discussion about translation. You are probably aware that the Bible is the most translated book in the world. According to the International Bible Society, "There are currently 6,909 living languages in the world. At least one book of Scripture has been translated for 2,932 of these languages. The New Testament is available in 1,333 languages, with portions in 1,045. The complete Bible has been translated into 553 languages." Translating a book as complex as the Bible, however, isn't an easy task. There are literally thousands of complete and partial, Hebrew and Greek manuscripts to choose from, and we don't know which ones are correct since none are identical. Rather than getting bogged down with a detailed discussion about the various manuscripts, which is much too complex to cover in this book, let's focus on the two translation processes: 1) The *translation approach*: word-for-word, meaning-for-meaning (also called thought-for-thought), or paraphrased, and 2) the *language translation*.

Translation Approach

Within the three translation approaches, there are over sixty *English language* versions of the Bible! We will look at the three approaches in order, from what is considered to be the most accurate to the least accurate process. Arguably the most popular is the King James Version (KJV), an example of the *word-for-word* translation approach. The advantage of this approach is that being the most literal translation, it attempts to mirror the original text as closely as possible. The downside is that it makes the English translation itself a bit more challenging to read. Multiple sources claim, however, that when compared to manuscripts found after the KJV was translated, such as the Dead Sea Scrolls, the KJV in its entirety is over ninety-eight percent "pure" or accurate. When analyzing just the New Testament, it is believed that where variations do exist, the basic meaning is seldom affected. Although the Old Testament is also considered trustworthy, scholars suggest consulting with other Bible versions, which typically rectifies any discrepancies.

A *meaning-for-meaning* translation approach, as found in the New International Version and the New English Version, is best for those seeking an easier read, especially with regard to studying the narrative portions of the Bible. When using this approach, however, the translator plays a significant role because his/her interpretation and doctrinal belief naturally influence the process. In addition, many people believe that the literal approach is best when dealing with the more conceptual books of the Bible, such as the epistles of Paul, which require greater accuracy.

The third translation approach, *paraphrasing*, is used in the Living Bible and The Message. These versions make the text even easier to read and thus, more accessible to the audience. A paraphrased version is also helpful when the reader seeks to understand the flow of a story. However, it is not considered ideal for determining the specific meaning of a passage. In these versions, the translators take even more liberty with the text, which can be seen by some as a huge disadvantage.

When considering the various Bible versions, there are a few points to keep in mind. First, the fact that these translation techniques range from *most accurate* to *least accurate* assumes the position that none are or can be 100 percent accurate. Second, most Bible scholars admit that it is best to consult multiple Bible versions when studying scripture, again implying that no single Bible version can be relied upon for complete accuracy. Third, a good number of Bible readers will naturally gravitate toward the easier-to-read versions in order to better understand the tenets of their faith. However, in so doing, they are placed in a Catch-22. The easier-to-read version is less accurate, but the accuracy of the KJV is a moot point if the reader can't decipher the text.

This information helped me to understand why a formal church service might use the KJV, while my Bible study pre-ferred the Living Bible. Again, however, I was faced with the knowledge that someone else (this time, a translator) was doing much of the interpretation for me. Everything I learned seemed to reinforce the idea that I needed to rely on my internal compass—my personal relationship with God—to interpret the Bible. But there was even more to this translation issue.

Language Translation

Once the translation approach is decided upon, translators face the arduous task of converting Hebrew and Greek manuscripts into English (or any number of other languages). Think about how challenging it is for us today to translate a written passage from Spanish (a Romance language), or German (a non-Romance language) into English, not to mention translating from a language that uses an entirely different writing system, like Chinese, Arabic, or Russian. Imagine how much more difficult is it to translate 3,000 year old Hebrew and 2,000 year old Greek, both with distinctive alphabets, into modern day English.

According to Dr. Joel Hoffman, a teacher, translator, and award-winning author of *The Bible Doesn't Say That: 40 Biblical Mistranslations, Misconceptions, and Other Misunderstandings*, the Bible contains quite a few errors of translation stemming from techniques that are inherently flawed and hundreds of years old. Dr. Hoffman explains that there are three common and problematic methods of deciphering the ancient words of the Bible: etymology, internal structure, and cognates. Further, he says, two other issues seriously hinder the Bible translation process: a misunderstanding of metaphor translation and an overall hesitation about changing historical translations at all. A complete discussion of this topic is beyond the scope of this book. What follows, therefore, are a few examples of how these issues impact the meaning of scripture.

Etymology refers to a word's origin. The fact that two words share the same source, however, doesn't mean that they share a similar meaning. For example, the word *ballot* comes from the Italian word *ballota* which refers to a small ball used to register a vote. The word *bullet* comes from the French word *boulet,* which also means a small ball. In spite of their similar origin, these two words—ballot and bullet—are not at all similar in meaning today. Another way to determine a word's meaning is through its internal structure, by analyzing its root, prefix, suffix, and so forth. However, it isn't difficult to find examples of words that aren't definable with this method. For example, an officer is not necessarily "one who works in an office", and you won't find naked people at a strip mall. Finally, in some cases, words, called cognates, are descendants from the same language. This causes problems because they look alike but don't share a similar meaning. For instance, the French word *demand* means "to ask," not "to demand." Even though these two words—the French word *demand* and the English word *demand*—are identical, we cannot automatically assume they mean the same thing.

Dr. Hoffman believes that we are better equipped today, more than at any other time in history, to accurately translate the ancient words of scripture. In spite of our new knowledge, however, these updated techniques haven't yet been used in any published Bible translations. This is perhaps due to a general resistance to change, which can occur in any field, but which is particularly evident in conservative religion. Here is just one example of why this resistance is problematic: 400 years ago when the KJV was written, "respect" meant "to be partial to, or to favor". This single piece of information drastically changes the meaning of Proverbs 28:21, which reads "to have respect of persons is not good". The point is that readers of the KJV today are at a disadvantage if not kept abreast of the various translational updates. Moreover, this specific example relates to the current translation of 400-year-old English text, not the difficulties surrounding the translation of ancient Greek and Hebrew manuscripts, which can result in even more significant errors of translation.

So Now What?

The Bible has had, and continues to have, a profoundly positive impact on people all over the world. For thousands of years human beings have sought, within its pages, the answers to life itself! Unfortunately, the Bible has also been subject to misinterpretation, leading to differences in doctrine (at best), and outright conflict (at worst). The reasons for this are many, and this chapter has only outlined a few, the intent of which is to demonstrate the importance of *personal* reflection. What is God telling *us, specifically*? As Rev. Wolsey suggested, we must go within and seek our own Truth. Practice Christian contemplation if you will. Read, explore, and wrestle not only with God's Word but with the spiritual topics found within this book. Come to your own conclusions. Since this is a personal journey, the conclusions you draw may not be the same as your neighbor. They may not be the same as your parents, your pastor, or your best friend. But that's OK!

As Rev. Thorpe explained, not only do we have the *right* to investigate—we have a *responsibility*! We owe it to ourselves to uncover those spiritual practices that nourish our souls, heal our bodies and minds, and help us to draw closer to God. Until now, that was easier said than done. A second search on Amazon will reveal that there are not many, if any, books designed to help Christians navigate the multitude of non-traditional spiritual practices that exist AND fit them into their Christian framework. It is my hope that this book will assist you in that endeavor by giving you the information you need and the courage to explore.

As you explore, I'd like you to view each of these practices as a potential item for your toolbox. Like any tool, which is neither inherently good nor bad, these individual practices are not, in and of themselves, good or bad. They *just are*. As with any tool, it is the user who determines how to apply it. For example, a knife, in the hands of a skilled surgeon is a tool that can save lives, a tool of great value! In the hands of a murderer, however, it is a tool of destruction. Perhaps it seems obvious, but the knife *itself* is neutral. It is the one who wields the knife that gives it purpose and meaning. In the same way, the tools in this book find their meaning through the one who practices them. When used to facilitate a connection to and a relationship with God, from a place of love, these tools can have amazing results!

Let us remember that as Christians—as *human beings*—we are united by Love. Our very *essence* is Love. Whether we acknowledge it or not, we have come to planet Earth to learn how to love and be loved, unconditionally. Keep this in mind as you explore, and you will never be led astray.

Part One: Self-Discovery

"At the center of your being, you have the answer; you know who you are and you know what you want."
Lao Tzu

"When I discover who I am, I'll be free."
Ralph Ellison, *Invisible Man*

I want to talk about self-discovery first, because it is the foundation of all other practices. It requires us to take a journey . . . *a
journey within.* We must first venture inside of ourselves before we
can effectively and authentically interact with our world. In my
experience, most folks don't dedicate a lot of time to nurturing a
relationship with themselves; many outright avoid it for fear of
what they will uncover. What if, after spending time with ourselves, we don't like us very much? Ignorance is bliss, right? The
thing is, discovering who we truly are is the only path toward
self-love. What's more, we can never truly love others until we
know and love ourselves—flaws and all. It is only after a sincere
voyage of self-discovery that we are able to release fear, let go of
judgment, and stand in our own authority, free to live an authentic life.

Cultivating Courage

Courage is one of the most fundamental gifts that we can
give ourselves. I think it was Maya Angelou who said that without it, we will consistently struggle to live a virtuous life. For that
reason, she says, courage is the first and most important of all
virtues. Obviously, living courageously is not a cake walk. All of
us, simply because we are human, must overcome a certain
amount of fear during our lifetimes. Yes, life can be scary! But
courage doesn't mean we must become completely fearless. In
fact, a certain amount of fear is healthy. Fear can keep us safe. It
can motivate us out of complacency. Too much fear, though,

stifles and stagnates. It contributes to daily stress. We develop a level of tension that becomes so commonplace that we rarely even notice it—but our bodies notice it. Stress is a common contributor to a host of physical ailments. I would argue as well, though, that fear-based stress, especially when it prevents us from living an authentic life, also chips away at our spirit and affects our relationships—the relationship we have with ourselves, with others, and with God. Again, the goal isn't to eliminate all fear—the goal is to act *in spite of our fear*. That's courage.

I vividly remember specific moments in my life when I had the choice to act or speak out or to stay quiet and small, allowing my fear to keep me stuck. The following story is one of my earliest and most profound moments of choice on my path to awakening (defined as becoming aware that I am a spiritual being having a physical experience).

While immersed in the Methodist church back in Texas, it was suggested to Bill that he look into joining a group of Christian business and professional men called the Gideons. You've probably heard of them; one of their missions is placing Bibles in hotel rooms. Because it is an all-male organization, there is also a women's auxiliary group, comprised of the Gideon members' wives. So, one evening, Bill and I attended an informational meeting to learn more about the organization and sign up, if we felt so led. I was ushered into an adjoining room to hear from the wives and read over their statement of beliefs, which I would have to sign in order to join. As I studied the document, a list of about ten faith statements that most Christians would readily agree with, my eyes froze midway down the page. Although I can't remember the exact wording, the sentence affirmed a belief in hell. I stopped reading. A mild panic set in as I frantically scrambled to come up with the words to describe why I wouldn't, couldn't, sign this document. I glanced up into the faces of these pleasant women who were staring at me, excited that I was going to join their ranks, probably thinking that signing this document was just a minor formality.

By this time, even though I was still very much involved in the Christian church, my belief system had significantly changed from that of my fellow parishioners. I no longer believed in hell, or any type of eternal damnation for that matter. I believed that the souls of *all* people would be reunited with God upon the death of their physical bodies. Reminiscent of Bill Clinton's "don't ask, don't tell" policy, as long as I didn't voice these newfound beliefs, I could retain my good standing in the church and keep my circle of friends. But now, as I sat with pen in hand, staring at the piece of paper in front of me, I was faced with a decision—to stand courageously in my Truth or to allow fear to, once again, dictate my actions. Until now, I had not been presented with a blatant forced choice like this. It was one thing to keep my mouth shut but quite another to outright deny (or lie about) my beliefs. As you've probably guessed by now, I gently and politely explained that I could not, in good faith, agree to each statement on their document and therefore, would not be joining the women's auxiliary. Although I still had a long way to go in terms of living an authentic life, I knew that I had crossed a threshold that night.

As we unpack this thing called *fear*, it is critically important to realize that a good number of our fears are not really *our* fears. For example, watch the nightly news on any given evening and you will be provided with a laundry list of things to be afraid of—the weather, bombs from rogue countries, the Republicans, the Democrats. In fact, I laughed out loud recently at one clip in particular. A news anchor was interviewing a reporter in the field about some potential disaster—a disaster that in all likelihood had a minimal possibility of occurring. The anchor, in a deeply concerned voice, asks:

"Should we be afraid?" (Apparently, the reporter hadn't conveyed his message frighteningly enough for the audience.)

"Yes," the reporter replied. "You should be very afraid!"

In this case, it wasn't enough to describe the fear-based event—they literally *told* their audience to be afraid. The entertainment industry feeds our fear, as well! As long as action movies have been in existence, humans have had to fight off alien invaders or other evil entities. The message is always, *kill or be killed!*

This culture of fear begins early on. As children, we are bombarded by (well-intentioned) messages, such as:

Stay close to mommy or you might be kidnapped by a stranger!

Put down that stick! You're gonna poke your eye out!

I confess. I've said some of these same things to my own children. It is easy to fall prey to our fears, particularly when it comes to those we love. And, what about the more subtle fear-based messages we receive from the media? These can be even more insidious because they are less overt:

Getting older? You're doomed to suffer from shingles, prostate cancer, low testosterone, dementia, (fill in the blank)!

Perhaps you should worry about your standing in the neighborhood. After all, John just bought a new (car, lawnmower, boat, golf cart).

In other words, people promote fear for many purposes, not the least of which are to control, sell, or entertain. We are saturated—marinated—in this fear, so much so that we can no longer distinguish between what's real and what's concocted by others to suit their own agenda. Learning to identify and release this fear—cultivating courage—is critical to the process of self-discovery.

Releasing Judgment

Much of the fear-based baggage we carry around takes the form of judgment. We fear what others will think or say about us. Be honest, how many times have you allowed others to control your actions because you were worried about what they might think? Have you ever judged another parent who:

Didn't breast-feed?

Used spanking as a form of discipline?

Refused to immunize their child?

In spite of what the Bible says about judgment (judge not!), humans are pretty darn good at it. The fear of judgment can literally paralyze us. Interestingly, though, we are often our own harshest critics. If I could spend the day with you, notebook in hand, writing down all of the things you say to yourself, would there be more positive or negative comments on the paper? Some of the things we say to ourselves we wouldn't say out loud to our worst enemy. We seem to enjoy beating ourselves up:

Why can't I stick to a diet? I'm ashamed of myself and have no will-power.

I keep hurting the ones that I love with my quick temper. Why am I such a bad person?

Why can't I find a loving partner? I must be unlovable.

Human beings have a difficult time accepting our own humanness. We seem to believe that we can somehow attain perfection, so we hold ourselves to impossible standards. And because we haven't accepted our own flaws, we certainly can't accept the flaws in others. To add insult to injury, the Christian church teaches us that we are *born* sinners, unworthy—that we will one day face judgment from the big man Himself. No wonder we are so full of self-loathing! In essence, we saturate ourselves with these judgmental messages and then spend years in therapy trying to repair our self-esteem.

It's no surprise, then, that we are afraid to look inward. The good news is, we do have value and worth. After all, we were made in God's image! The Bible tells us that if we seek, we will find what we are looking for. But the seeking comes first. And seeking without judgment is the only way we can truthfully investigate our internal landscape.

Living Authentically

A journey of self-discovery offers us the opportunity to re-create ourselves based on a set of principles that accurately reflect our inner nature. It allows us to reflect on and adjust our belief system based on who we are, rather than on who others think we should be. It takes self-love.

It's difficult to stand up for our beliefs when we don't know what we believe. Don't get me wrong. Most of us are like pit bulls when it comes to defending our position. We will happily march against Monsanto, picket abortion clinics, or defend our political candidate. But positions don't equal beliefs. Sometimes, we simply argue our point out of habit or to maintain the status quo. What's more, many of our so-called beliefs are not even ours! Naturally, our parents are the first people to start to influence our belief system. Once we hit school, we begin to mimic our friends and learn from our teachers. As we grow older, the media starts to impact our decision-making. Before we know it, we've created an entire belief system that may or may not reflect *who we really are.* At that point, we're often too afraid to investigate, to figure out if our core beliefs really resonate with our inner being, because then we might have to do something about it.

For me, it wasn't that I was afraid of the investigation. In fact, I often reflected on the external messages that didn't ring true, particularly those of my church leaders. But after questioning my priest at camp that day, exposing my vulnerability and being shut down, I learned that there were unpleasant consequences to leading an authentic life. Of course, at thirteen I didn't really understand the concept of authenticity. What I understood loud and clear was fear. Fear of standing out, fear of speaking my truth, fear of being judged. Sadly, it took the better part of forty years to conquer that fear.

The first step, then, in an authentic spiritual journey, the first step toward cultivating a closer relationship with our God, our creator, is exploring our own inner landscape. Like an onion, we must peel away the layers of conditioning, the layers of other people's ideas about who we are. We could also use the analogy of a geode. Little by little, we must chip away at the hard outer crust that we've fashioned to protect the beautiful gemstone inside—a crust of doubt, fear, loathing, jealousy, judgment, and anger. Have you ever cracked a geode? It's not easy! In the same way, it's not a cakewalk to hammer away at the shell that surrounds and protects the core of our being. No wonder we busy ourselves, day after day, running from here to there until we flop back into bed, too exhausted to reflect on the day. No wonder we numb ourselves with the drug of our choice. The problem with avoidance, though, is that we miss out on a loving relationship with ourselves, and by default, God.

So, what's the answer? First, we must sit with ourselves and silence the outside voices until we can hear our own. This takes time. We have become conditioned to listening to others, squelching our own inner voice until we can no longer distinguish it from the pack. Practicing the techniques in this section can help us turn down the noise level of the outside world long enough to detect our own inner wisdom.

How to Begin Self-discovery

Not only is self-discovery challenging, it takes time. In fact, it is a lifelong process. Every encounter, every experience has the potential to reveal new insight about what makes us tick. Even on our deathbed, we have the opportunity to reflect and discover aspects of ourselves that had previously been hidden. If I were to ask you for the first word that comes to mind when you think about this process of self-discovery—going within—you'd probably respond with an emphatic—*meditation*! How many times have you heard that you *have* to meditate to be spiritual, that meditation is the best way (or the *only* way) to connect with ourselves? While I would agree that meditation is an important practice, I would add two caveats: 1) meditation isn't the only way to discover ourselves and 2) meditation isn't just about sitting still and being quiet. As you read through the chapters in this section, not only will you gain clarity on what meditation is and what it isn't, you will learn several other techniques that can shed light on who you are and why you are here.

Chapter 3 - Meditation

When you think about the word *meditation*, what do you envision? Most folks picture someone sitting cross-legged on the floor, eyes closed, back straight, hands with palms facing up and resting on the knees, maybe even with the thumb and middle finger forming a circle. You might imagine this person intoning a mantra, like *Om*, his mind completely devoid of any wayward, intruding thoughts, like *Ouch, my leg is falling asleep!* or *I think my car is due for an oil change.* Suddenly, the meditator's body starts to vibrate in pure ecstasy, becoming *one with everything,* virtually exploding with a love that must now be shared with all of humanity! Ok, maybe I exaggerated the last part just a little, but did I come close to describing your idea of the perfect meditative experience? Well, sometimes meditation looks like that, but it doesn't have to. The scenario above is often the reason we stop before we even get started. So, what is meditation if it's not sitting quietly on the floor waiting for something profound to happen?

What is Meditation?

There are many different types of meditation, with roots in almost every major religion, a testament to its value as a spiritual practice. Buddhists practice Zen (Zazen), Vipassana, and Metta meditation, while you might find a Hindi engaged in Transcendental or Mantra meditation. Although it is not typically called meditation, the Christian practice of Contemplation, or "sitting with God," is closely aligned with the process and purpose of some forms of meditation. Typically, meditation involves focused attention; for example, attending to (or being *mindful* of) your breath, a phrase or affirmation, a sound or chant, or a particular task. Meditation does not have to involve being still—moving meditative practices, such as Qigong, Tai Chi, and Yoga, will be covered in more detail in the next two chapters. In spite of its association with spirituality, meditation doesn't have to fall under any particular religious practice. In fact, some meditation proponents claim it is actually a science, with specific principles and concrete, research-based results.

One of these proponents is Jon Kabat-Zinn, PhD, founding executive director of the Center for Mindfulness in Medicine, Health Care, and Society at the University of Massachusetts Medical School and the founding director of its renowned Stress Reduction Clinic. Kabat-Zinn practices and teaches a research-based form of meditation called Mindfulness Based Stress Reduction (MBSR). MBSR helps transform our minds through the identification of negative habits and thought patterns. We learn to see things as they are, including ourselves—our feelings, our thoughts, and our experiences. The increased awareness that arises through mindfulness meditation can help us reduce stress and alter these undesirable thought patterns, resulting in enhanced clarity, positivity, and peace. According to Kabat-Zinn this process occurs through *purposeful attention* to the *present moment* in a *non-judgmental* manner. Before we move on, let's unpack that last sentence.

What does it mean to engage in *purposeful attention*? It means that we give our full focus to the task at hand, whether that is washing the dishes, eating, gardening, or just sitting quietly. In a mindfulness meditation the attention is on the breath. During a meal, it might mean that we pay attention to each bite, engaging all of our senses in order to experience and appreciate the food in a new way. A purposeful walk through the woods might reveal sounds, sights, feelings, or smells that we never noticed before.

What does the *present moment* have to do with it? Well, when you think about it, there really isn't anything else BUT the present moment. After all, the future is not yet here, and when it does get here, it will be the *now*. The past is behind us, no longer in our *now*. In fact, life is simply a series of *present moments*, strung together like a gigantic movie reel. And each of those moments is a gift.

Zen Master Thich Nhat Hanh, a Buddhist monk and peace activist, often relates his dishwashing story as a way to illustrate this idea of *living in the now*. In his book, *At Home in the World, Stories and Essential Teachings from a Monk's Life*, he describes this much-maligned chore as something we attempt to rush through in order to get on with a more enjoyable activity, such as eating dessert, for example. But, as we sit down to eat our dessert, our mind jumps to what we intend to do after dessert. Before we know it, the cake is gone, and we don't even remember how it tasted. In other words, when we are preoccupied with the memories of the past or the expectations of the future, we miss out on the joy of living *now*, moment by moment. When we give our full attention to the task at hand, even if that task is washing the dishes, we can learn to appreciate even the most mundane moments of our lives. We come to understand our lives as sacred—every moment, every activity.

The *judgment* piece we covered a few paragraphs ago. The reason Kabat-Zinn includes it in his description of mindfulness, however, is because when we slow down, eliminate distractions, and pay attention, we can no longer hide from ourselves. This is when things start to get real, maybe even real scary. In MBSR, the goal is to understand that although intruding thoughts will pop in, we can observe them without judgment and allow them to float on by. Then, we just bring our attention back to the breath. And yes, we might have to do this over and over again, at least until we get better at holding our focus. Understand, too, that some of those pesky thoughts might be unpleasant—negative self-talk, sad memories, or even feelings of anger—but remember, we are learning to love ourselves as God loves us, flaws and all. Discovering who we are is the first step in the self-love process, and that's what meditation can help us with.

How it Works

There are hundreds of meditation techniques designed to fit all sorts of personalities and lifestyles. One of my favorite places to start is the Palouse Mindfulness website, which offers a free, eight-week online course developed by Dave Potter, a retired psychotherapist trained in MBSR by Jon Kabat-Zinn. This program introduces participants to several different types of mindful and meditative processes, including those that focus on compassion, sensory experience, and movement, as well as those designed to alleviate physical or emotional pain. The Palouse Mindfulness program can help you identify which type of meditation is most appropriate for you.

There are many other ways to learn how to meditate. Look for books, videos, or recordings by popular teachers like Sharon Salzberg, Pema Chodron, Tara Brach, and Jonathan Foust. Guided meditations, in particular, are great for those who are left-brained or overwhelmed by intruding thoughts. If you don't want to listen to someone narrating the meditation but don't want to sit in silence either, you can listen to a recording of soothing music or mantra chanting. It can also help to recite the mantra along with the recording, as the vibration created can be very relaxing to the mind and the body. For those who prefer to practice meditating with others, a quick Google search may provide a list of meditation classes or groups in your area, some of which are even free or donation-based.

Whatever you do, don't give up! Like any new skill, meditation takes time and practice. Remember, meditation is not about getting rid of all thought—it is the understanding that we are *more* than our thoughts. We are the thinker behind the thoughts.

How it Can Help

Based on a research summary compiled by the University of Massachusetts Medical School, meditation is a powerful component of a comprehensive, whole health plan. Studies have demonstrated that MBSR can significantly and positively affect disorders such as coronary artery disease, hypertension, cancer, chronic pain, depression and anxiety, multiple sclerosis, and many other health issues. In addition, MBSR has been shown to increase one's quality of life and overall sense of well-being. Makes sense, right? Logically, your quality of life is going to suffer if you're mired in pain, illness, depression, or stress. That meditation can have such a huge impact on our physical body is icing on the cake. For the purposes of this book, however, we also want to investigate how meditation can lead to self-knowledge and by default, self-love, which is the source of true happiness and well-being.

Soon after birth, human beings begin to form an identity (our ego self) that is largely defined by external criteria. As children, we identify with our name, age, and gender, maybe even our grade level in school. As adults, we begin to define ourselves as mother, father, student, spouse, supervisor, activist, educator, cancer survivor, triathlete, and so on. These labels not only define us, they come to represent our imagined value as an individual—a description of our contribution to the world. They serve as a source of self-esteem...until they don't. At some point, many of us hit a wall, usually around midlife (hence the term, *midlife crisis*). We start questioning our purpose, the meaning of life, perhaps even our very identity. This can be frightening! If we no longer define ourselves through these various external labels, who exactly are we? And, if we do discover a new person—the *real* person—under all of those labels, how will others react? Will we be accepted? Will we be ridiculed? Why do I care? Should I care? How can I *not* care?

Herein lies the beauty of the meditative process. Meditation creates the time and space to contemplate those questions, to peel off all of the exterior labels until we arrive at the internal (eternal) core—the truth of who we are. When we muster the courage to engage in this process without judgment, we can begin to accept ourselves...our strengths and our imagined weaknesses. Eventually, we come to realize that we have no weaknesses. *All* of our attributes can be used for our own highest good and in service to others. Further, our value as a human being doesn't depend on anyone else's definition or description; we are not the sum total of our accomplishments. Meditation, in whatever form we choose, can help us appreciate this eternal truth.

Chapter 4 - Moving Meditation: Qigong and Tai Chi

As mentioned in the previous chapter, meditation is all about focused attention, and as Thich Nhat Hanh's story demonstrated, meditation doesn't have to mean sitting still. Let's face it, sometimes we have a hard time paying attention unless our body is distracted. That is why fidget toys were created for school children. It's why we find ourselves tapping our toe, drumming our fingers, or flipping a pencil while engaged in an otherwise-passive activity requiring our attention. Human bodies are built to move. Luckily, we can still develop a healthy meditative practice even if we are not good at sitting still.

Truthfully, mindfulness can take place—indeed, should take place—all the time, no matter the activity. We gain more from life when we are fully present. That being said, there are certain activities we can engage in that are specifically designed to be meditative in nature. Coloring has exploded as an adult pastime that many find relaxing. Moreover, artistic endeavors, in general, have the added bonus of opening up our creative side (engaging our right brains), allowing for an influx of inspiration and insight, a pleasant byproduct of meditation. Walking a labyrinth is another form of moving meditation that can create the opportunity for a profound experience.

Even hobbies like cooking or gardening can transport us into a meditative state when we become so engrossed in them, so laser focused, that we *get lost* in the moment. Have you ever found yourself so absorbed in a pleasurable activity that you didn't hear someone speaking to you? Or you finally looked up to realize that what seemed like five minutes was really five hours? That's because while you were actively engaged, your mind was actually in the space of no-time, where time seems to stand still. It's the same thing we experience when we zone out while driving and end up at home, with no recollection of the actual drive. In all of those cases, we have entered a meditative state. And you thought meditation was difficult, right?

Two of the most well-known moving meditation practices are Qigong and Tai Chi. This chapter will focus on those practices in more detail.

What is Qigong?

Qigong (pronounced *chi gong*) is a series of bodily movements that makes use of the life force energy (Qi) that flows throughout our body. In Qigong, the movements are stationary rather than flowing, like they are in Tai Chi, and each solitary movement is repeated a certain number of times. Qigong is also more specific; there are certain movements for certain situations, as opposed to Tai Chi, which combines a series of flowing movements tied together in sequence. For example, there is a specific Qigong move that helps open the lungs. A practitioner might choose to work on that movement until the energy is flowing freely again and then choose another movement. Meditation has always been an important part of a Qigong practice, as it is the mind that directs and regulates the energy movement throughout the body and allows the practitioner to sense the movement of these subtle energies. Unfortunately, many current forms of Qigong have virtually eliminated this critical piece—the systematic, internal activation and management of the Qi-energy.

Although there have been references to Qigong as far back as 5,000 years ago, its history has only been documented for the past 2,500 years. In fact, the actual term *Qigong* wasn't in general use until the twentieth century. From about 200 B.C. through 500 A.D., Buddhism and yoga, which had been brought from India into China, intersected with Taoism, creating the philosophical foundation for what would eventually become Qigong. However, the practices were kept secret and passed down to only a select few. Around 500 A.D., a Buddhist monk named Bodhidarma married the spiritual and martial arts branches of Qigong and began teaching the techniques to fellow monks and martial artists. The continued air of secrecy surrounding Qigong, however, meant that thousands of different styles were eventually created. Unique styles existed not only within individual families and villages but within each religious or martial arts group, as well. These styles, with their quirky names, include Animal Frolics, Eight Pieces of Brocade, Swimming Dragon, and Six Syllable Secret.

Qigong was long considered to be a part of Chinese medicine, and many physicians were, in fact, Qigong masters who offered Qigong as their treatment of choice, using it to restore balance to their patient's energy field. Over time, as Western influences and technology infiltrated China, Qigong (and Chinese medicine in general) became the subject of much research and scientific study. In 1985, the China Qigong Science Association was created, and the positive health benefits of Qigong became more widely disseminated. Throughout the 1990s, Qigong earned worldwide recognition, and by 1997 there were over 100,000 practitioners beyond the borders of China. Qigong's reputation as a healing modality has only continued to increase, and at present, it remains one of the most popular forms of exercise in the world.

What is Tai Chi?

If you have ever seen someone, perhaps in a park, moving their body in a slow, rhythmic fashion, you may have been watching a Tai Chi session. A *gentle* form of Chinese martial arts, Tai Chi is not only easy to learn but extremely healthy for body, mind, and spirit. The ancient Chinese philosophy of Taoism, which stresses the natural balance of all things, formed the foundation of Tai Chi over 3,000 years ago. In Taoism, it is believed that two opposite but complimentary energies—yin and yang—work together, in harmony with all things in life, creating perpetual balance. Therefore, within the flowing sequences of

Tai Chi, some movements are soft and pliant, like the *yin*, or feminine energy, while others are hard and rigid, which is associated with the *yang*, or masculine energy. One of the primary principles of Tai Chi is mindfulness, seeking to control one's breath and physical movement while remaining in the here and now. In a non-religious sense, Tai Chi can be considered a spiritual experience; many practitioners find that it even becomes a way of life.

It is believed that Tai Chi emerged as a specific style of Qigong. Over time, numerous styles of Tai Chi have also arisen, based on the particular form of the founding practitioner. As far as reliable sources can determine, the oldest form of Tai Chi is the Chen Style, developed in the 1670s by Chen Wangting. It is characterized by its explosive power, low stances, and emphasis on spiral force. The Yang Style, created in the early twentieth century by Yang Lu-chan, is said to be the most popular, perhaps because of its gentle, graceful, slow movements, which are easy to learn. Wu Style (also called Hao Style) was created by Wu Yuxiang and then passed on to Hao Weizheng between the late nineteenth and early twentieth centuries. Practitioners of this form are known by their focus on internal power and correct positioning. A second Wu Style was founded by Wu Quan-you and his son, Wu Jian-quan, around this same time frame and is said to be pleasant to watch and rich in techniques. The youngest of all Tai Chi forms is the Sun Style, created by Sun Lu-tang in the early twentieth century. This form is enjoyed for its efficacy and safety, allowing the practitioner to feel the flow of Qi more quickly. The Sun Style utilizes higher stances, which are beneficial to older practitioners, and is more compact, meaning that it can be practiced in smaller spaces. With over 300 million participants, Tai Chi has become one of the most popular exercises today and is practiced in almost every corner of the world.

How they Work

In both Qigong and Tai Chi, the breath and body movements stimulate *Qi*, the subtle, life force energy that animates all living things. This energy flows through channels in the body called *meridians*, keeping them unblocked, since energy blockages can manifest as physical or emotional disorders. (The body's energy system is discussed in more detail in part three). In addition, both Qigong and Tai Chi are meditative in nature, which harnesses the power of being in the *now*.

You don't have to be in great shape—overly strong, balanced, or flexible—to practice Qigong or Tai Chi. After all, the goal of these modalities is to develop those very skills. For this reason, both Qigong and Tai Chi are particularly beneficial for folks with restricted movement. Adapted or modified forms of the exercises can be done from a chair or bed, for example. There is no equipment required, and you can practice almost anywhere. Finding a personal class to attend is ideal, particularly for beginners. Prices will vary by location but should be similar to other martial arts classes that meet weekly. That being said, the movements can be learned at home by watching a video, and if the philosophical principles of these practices are important to you, they can be researched online or in a book. It is suggested, however, that new Tai Chi participants take time to watch and study the various styles before choosing one because the numerous forms can be overwhelming.

How they Can Help

Like all meditative practices, Qigong and Tai Chi enable us to transition into a state of tranquility, a space where we rise above the business of life and rest in the truth of who we are. By eliminating outside distractions and reducing stress, we have the opportunity to let go of the external sense of self in order to find our true essence. What makes moving meditation even better is the fact that because we are active, we can take advantage of a number of other health benefits. Studies have shown that Tai Chi can improve blood pressure and circulation, increase flexibility, balance, and muscle strength, bolster our immune system, reduce pain, improve posture and range of motion, and increase overall fitness. Qigong is known to enhance concentration and deep breathing, encourage cardiovascular and respiratory fitness, and stimulate the lymphatic system. The mental and emotional benefits of both practices include increased clarity and focus, reduced anxiety, stress, and depression, and improved sleep. Not surprisingly, all of these benefits have the potential to positively impact our overall quality of life.

Chapter 5 - Yoga

It's hard to deny it—yoga has definitely hit the mainstream. As I write these words, folks are practicing yoga with goats, cats, and dogs; on paddleboards, in pools, and in the snow (*hot yoga* has some competition). Believe it or not, there's even *naked* yoga. The numbers don't lie—yoga practitioners have increased from about four million in 2001 to twenty million in 2011, with no sign of slowing down. Part of yoga's appeal, particularly since the 1980s, has been the physical benefits it imparts. A consistent yoga practice can result in improved flexibility and range of motion, increased endurance, balance, and strength, and an enhanced immune system. Yoga can alleviate chronic pain and physical injuries, as well as the symptoms of depression and anxiety and has also been shown to positively impact diseases like diabetes and high blood pressure. Although the physical benefits are not to be discounted, yoga's true essence is about mind-body integration. Yoga literally means *to unite*.

Was I afraid of yoga? Of course! It has roots in Hinduism. And . . . well . . . Hinduism isn't Christianity. In spite of its surging popularity, for Christians, there is still a good bit of controversy surrounding its practice. As I understand it, the conflict surrounds the fact that Hindus pray to other Gods, which in the Christian faith is considered to be idol worship. Although Hindus do believe in one God, Brahman, the eternal

God and Creator of All, there are also "secondary" Gods, who serve to help people *find* the universal God. I also understand that in India, Hindus can be seen performing yoga poses in front of these God-statues. (Disclaimer: I've never been to India and have only heard this through other sources.) This would explain the Christian aversion to yoga—it has been linked with idol worship.

Necessity being the mother of invention, *Christian yoga* was developed. In classes like *Yaweh yoga* or *Holy yoga*, practitioners can focus specifically on Jesus or even scripture verses, while still benefiting from the breath work and poses. While Christian yoga can certainly serve as a pathway to self-discovery, leading to a stronger relationship with God, I would ask readers to examine their apprehension toward traditional yoga. Is it about fear? As I mentioned early on, I understand fear, but it's time to examine that fear and take baby steps outside of your comfort zone. Rather than take someone else's word for it, examine the belief for yourself.

What is Yoga?

In a sentence, yoga is a group of physical, mental, and spiritual practices or disciplines designed to lead the practitioner to self-awareness. Yoga's roots can be traced back to ancient India, but until the fifth century AD, it was a rather loosely defined religious and meditative practice. Once it took hold among

Hindus, Buddhists, and Jains, yoga became more of a spiritual practice that revolved around several core values or principles. These principles eventually shaped the various schools or traditions of yoga that emerged around 500-1500 AD, such as Bhakti, Tantra and Hatha. There is some debate regarding the number of schools that currently exist, but in addition to the previous three, most would also include Raja, Karma, Jnana, and Kriya. While the *schools* of yoga are based upon core values and spiritual principles, there have been an inordinate number of yoga practices that have arisen from those schools of thought, not the least of which include Bikram, Ashtanga, Kundalini, Vinyasa, and Yin yoga. Hatha yoga is now considered a generic term for any practice that combines body postures, breath work, and meditation and most closely aligns with what yoga looks like today.

Yoga finally arrived in the West during the mid-nineteenth century and was popularized by a Hindu monk, Swami Vivekananda, who traveled throughout Europe and the US to spread knowledge of Hinduism. The practice of Hatha yoga began in the U.S. around 1930, with a significant jump in popularity in the 1960s, once Hindu spirituality caught the attention of American youth. Once the physical health benefits of yoga were realized, its practice started to skyrocket, very often becoming separated from its meditative roots. But it is the meditative aspect—a spiritual rather than religious focus—that gives yoga the power to increase self-awareness, calm the mind, and expand our consciousness.

How it Works

Because there are so many varieties of yoga, you are almost guaranteed to find a class that meets you where you are, regardless of your fitness level, comfort level, time availability or budget. Yoga is also a practice that can be done in groups, for those who prefer camaraderie, or individually, for those who value privacy. If price is an issue, one idea is to invest in six to eight weeks of classes, long enough to learn a few basic poses, and then practice at home with a friend. Gaia television is another option, since so many of us have moved to subscription-based, a la carte television. Gaia is relatively inexpensive and has tons of alternative options, including all sorts of yoga programs. Of course, there is a plethora of books and videos that can help. If the goal is self-discovery (which it probably is or you wouldn't be reading this book), be sure to seek out a teacher or practice that focuses on the spiritual and meditative aspects of yoga.

How it Can Help

Touched on briefly above, yoga was founded on several core principles. According to The Chopra Center, they are as follows:

Law of Pure Potentiality: The true essence of everything in our world, including us, is pure consciousness—the energy of awareness. We are spiritual beings temporarily housed in a physical body.

Law of Giving and Receiving: Keeping this life-force energy circulating within our world requires a balance of giving and receiving, an ebb and flow.

Law of Karma: Every action generates a balanced reaction; what we give, we receive.

Law of Least Effort: When we offer no resistance to life, good or bad, we can more easily tap into the infinite power of the universe.

Law of Intention and Desire: When we tap into the infinite power of the universe, through our loving intentions, we can manifest our desires effortlessly.

Law of Detachment: When we release our desire for a specific outcome, we allow the power of the universe to work its magic.

Law of Dharma: True fulfillment comes when we live our purpose. We must seek within to discover this purpose and then lovingly offer our gifts and talents to the world.

A yoga practice that is founded on these universal principles can help us discover our true essence, as well as the peace that comes from connecting with the Truth of who we are. As with other meditative practices, yoga provides the space/time in which to explore, while the poses (*Asanas*), breath work (*Pranayama*), and meditative intent (*Dharana*) allow us to focus on the present moment. As with other forms of moving meditation, keeping the body engaged can help us control our wandering mind, making it easier to concentrate. Another benefit of moving meditative practices, in general, is that we learn to cultivate a loving relationship with our physical body, which is often the target of judgment and negative self-talk. Moving meditations, therefore, serve to not only heal and strengthen the physical body but to also repair the damaged relationship between our physical and spiritual Selves. The physical body houses our internal essence, our Soul, so it is critical that we take care of and appreciate it.

Chapter 6 - Reincarnation and Past Life Exploration

Reincarnation was one of those concepts that I never really thought much about. I just assumed it was baloney (because that's what I was taught). Reincarnation is the idea that our soul experiences many incarnations in the physical realm, not just the life we are currently living. It is closely tied to the concept of karma, which is often perceived as a justification for reincarnation—to create balance (although most people believe it is related to justice and punishment). You've no doubt heard the phrase, *karma's a b*****, which implies that if you behave badly in this life, you can expect payback in the next. (That's not really an accurate description of karma, but I don't want to get off on a tangent here.)

For the longest time, I simply embraced Christianity's disbelief in reincarnation. After all, I had been taught that anything associated with Eastern philosophy was considered taboo and was incompatible with the Christian religion. As I started to reevaluate my belief system, however, it was another one of those ideas that I just couldn't reconcile. First of all, there are places in the Bible where it is written that those who had died (most notably, Jesus), subsequently reappeared—albeit in Spirit form—to the living. For example, after Jesus's death, "The tombs broke open and the bodies of many holy people who had died were raised to life. They came out of the tombs, and after

Jesus's resurrection they went into the holy city and appeared to many people" Matthew 27:52-53. In addition, there are specific verses that seem to presuppose a belief in reincarnation: ". . . when Melchizedek met Abraham, Levi was still in the body of his ancestor" (Hebrews 7:10) and "Naked I came from my mother's womb, and naked I shall return there" (Job 1:21).

Another interesting hypothesis held by some Biblical scholars and worthy of mention is the idea that a group of clergy members who met in Constantinople in AD 553 deliberately suppressed specific passages that supported the concept of reincarnation. Theorists suggest that this was done either to manipulate the masses (for a reason that isn't clear) or in response to what they called the "spiritual immaturity" of those early Christians, believing that they didn't have the ability to understand the doctrine at that time. Although this is a topic worth noting, it is much too broad for this book to cover in detail.

I think what ultimately convinced me, though, were the thousands of documented cases of children who have remembered past lives, compiled by researchers like Dr. Jim Tucker, author of *Life Before Life: A Scientific Investigation of Children's Memories of Previous Lives*. Dr. Tucker (who, incidentally, was raised a Southern Baptist) is a child psychiatrist and professor of psychiatry and neurobehavioral sciences at the University of Virginia School Of Medicine. His work builds on that of his

UVA colleague, the late Dr. Ian Stevenson, who, over the course of forty years, investigated 3,000 instances of past life memories and authored fourteen books on reincarnation. One of the most fascinating cases Tucker studied was that of child baseball prodigy, Christian Haupt, who, as a toddler, regaled his mother with tales of his "other" life as Hall of Famer Lou Gehrig. But this story had another layer of meaning for me. As Christian's mother, Cathy Byrd describes in her memoir, *The Boy Who Knew Too Much: An Astounding True Story of a Young Boy's Past-Life Memories*, her son's declarations challenged her Christian faith. After conducting her own biblically-based research, Cathy says she found nothing that made the concept of reincarnation incompatible with Christianity.

If one is open to the possibility of reincarnation, then it only takes a small leap to entertain the possibility that those past lives can be accessed and mined for information. The concepts of reincarnation and past life exploration burst into the mainstream when Dr. Brian Weiss, a Columbia University and Yale Medical School-trained psychiatrist, was featured on the Oprah Winfrey show. In 1980, Dr. Weiss was treating a patient named Catherine, who suffered from severe phobias that had not responded to traditional therapy. As a last resort, he tried hypnotherapy. It was during that session, and subsequent hypnosis sessions with Catherine, that Dr. Weiss came to the following realizations: 1) Reincarnation is real, 2) past lives could be remembered on some level, 3) these memories can impact our current life, and 4) past-life regression can miraculously heal trauma and illnesses that are resistant to traditional therapeutic intervention. The incredible story of Weiss, a skeptical psychiatrist, and Catherine, his young patient, is recounted in his best-selling book, *Many Lives, Many Masters: The True Story of a Prominent Psychiatrist, His Young Patient, and the Past-Life Therapy That Changed Both Their Lives.*

What is a Past Life Regression? (PLR)

PLR is an umbrella concept that describes any process, typically some form of hypnosis or guided meditation, by which a client is able to relax enough to access their subconscious mind (SC) without interference from the conscious mind (CM). In regression therapy, the purpose is to uncover the origin of a client's problem; however, there are many other reasons a person might choose to experience PLR. Connecting to one's SC can offer insight into many areas of life, including career, relationships, family, or health. Not only does our SC act as a storehouse of personal information, but because we are energetically connected to what psychologist Carl Jung called the Collective Unconscious (CU), we have access to much, much more!

Jung believed that the psyche of a human being was comprised of three inter-related systems: the ego, the personal unconscious, and the CU, a database of information that is shared with all other members of the human species. He theorized that the existence of this CU explained why certain universal images and thoughts consistently appeared across cultures, as evidenced in societal literature, art, and religion. The current understanding of PLR practitioners is that this CU is not just limited to the human race; it can be expanded to include the entire Quantum Field (QF), also called the Divine Mind, the Akashic Record, or The Book of Life. Therefore, although this process is commonly called PLR, the information accessed can extend beyond *just* the client's past lives.

In chapters 3, 4, and 5, I explained how a meditative state can help us get in touch with the internal (eternal) truth of who we are. Well, that internal *piece* is called the Higher Self (HS). It is our connection to the QF and to each other. The HS holds the key to the truth of who we are, including information about our current life, as well as any of our past lives. And, although it might sound surprising, the wisdom of our HS can be accessed *and communicated with* through the SC during experiences like PLR.

There are a number of modalities that employ PLR techniques. Arguably, one of the most well-known is Quantum Healing Hypnosis Technique® (QHHT), developed by Dolores Cannon, a hypnotherapist who, like Brian Weiss, stumbled upon the past life phenomenon in 1968, when PLR was virtually unheard of. Dolores passed in 2014 but left behind an incredible legacy of books and research spanning almost fifty years. Her

QHHT modality is still taught, under the leadership of her daughter, Julia. Other modalities that utilize some form of PLR include Beyond Quantum Healing (BQH), established by Candace Craw-Goldman, and Michael Newton's Life Between Lives® (LBL), as well as trainings conducted by Brian Weiss.

How it Works

Depending on the method and practitioner, a PLR session will generally last between two and eight hours and can take place in-person or online, via a videoconferencing program like Skype or Zoom (QHHT strictly prohibits online sessions, however). Clients are typically asked to bring in a list of questions that they would like to explore during the session. The first part of the appointment will involve a thorough interview to establish rapport and allow the practitioner to understand all aspects of the client's questions. In addition, this initial discussion should cover topics such as client history, managing expectations, logistics, and whether the session will be recorded. As a general rule, clients will want to dress comfortably, limit caffeine intake prior to the session, and eat a light snack before arrival.

During the regression portion of the appointment, the client will sit or lie down, while the practitioner guides the client into a deep trance or hypnotic state, similar to what is experienced just before falling asleep. This can take anywhere from ten to twenty minutes or more, depending upon the experience of the practitioner and the client's ability to relax. Once the client is relaxed, the practitioner will assist the client in accessing and investigating one or more past lives, after which, the SC will be contacted. Any of the client's questions that were not answered by way of the past life experiences can then be asked of the SC directly.

Once the practitioner has explored as many of the client's concerns as possible, s/he will guide the client back into an awakened state. The practitioner should answer any questions the client has about the experience, offer the client water, and provide a copy of the recording (if applicable). Prices for a PLR can vary widely, depending on such things as the practitioner's experience, the geographic area, and the overall demand for sessions. However, as a ballpark estimate, most PLR sessions will cost the same per hour as a massage, multiplied by the number of hours the session takes.

How it Can Help

During a PLR, we are going straight to the source for answers—our own SC/HS. For that reason, a session can have profound, life-changing results. Each session is unique, however. Results may take place immediately or may reveal themselves over the course of weeks, months, or even years. Experienced practitioners, such as Brian Weiss, Dolores Cannon, Candace Craw-Goldman, and Michael Newton, have documented thousands of cases (written about in their books and/or on their websites) in which clients were miraculously healed of physical and emotional disorders, including cancer, phobias, hearing loss, and more. The reason for this is that we can find out where the disorder originated and why—was there a lesson that we needed to learn, for instance? Tackling the core of an issue rather than simply treating symptoms results in true healing.

Aside from direct physical or emotional healing, though, the client acquires a more expanded perspective of life and his/her role in the universe. PLR allows us to understand what drives our choices, as well as the ramifications of those choices, particularly as they relate to those that we are in relationship with. We gain empathy and compassion for ourselves and others, as we uncover the roles we play in each incarnation. PLR can help us through times of crisis by revealing the lessons behind the obstacles we face. And perhaps most importantly, we discover that we are never alone. We are inextricably connected to ALL THAT IS, and we are loved unconditionally!

In the summer of 2018, I was guided to become a BQH practitioner myself. Although I have not practiced for very long, relative to the pioneers mentioned above, I have witnessed profound changes in my own clients. In all honesty, I'm not entirely clear, from a scientific standpoint, how this process works, but I'm OK with that. Given what I've experienced in my first year as a BQH practitioner, I know there is a lot more to this universe than meets the eye; science just needs to catch up! The good news is—science is getting there. Quantum physicists are starting to find evidence for many spiritual principles, including the idea that we are all united within the Quantum Field, mentioned earlier in this chapter. Again, it's all about exploration—being willing to step out of our comfort zone in the anticipation of a greater reward: a better understanding of ourselves and our world.

Chapter 7 - Astrology

For the longest time, perhaps not unlike many of my readers, I operated under the assumption that Astrology was simply a pseudoscience that was, again, frowned upon by Christians. I imagined Astrologers as charlatans, all decked out in their gauzy clothing and headdresses, providing *readings* to help folks part with their money. But, when we dive deeply into its history and explore the modern day practice of Astrology, we uncover an ancient discipline that can offer us a more complete picture of ourselves and our lives.

Astrology is one of those subjects that everyone seems to know a little something about. Typically, it's seen as a harmless way to learn about ourselves and others and maybe even predict the success of our relationships. It can even be a great conversation starter. The layperson's breath of knowledge probably includes, at the very least, the twelve zodiac signs and their (often stereotypical) strengths and weaknesses. A Scorpio (my sign), for example, has a reputation for being loyal but vindictive. Ask around, and you'll probably also hear that Scorpios are passionate lovers that you don't want to cross. On the other hand, we're also prone to spiritual transformation—no coincidence, given this book project. Undoubtedly, you've also heard the phrase, *Watch out! Mercury's in retrograde!* often used as an excuse for everything from computer problems to relationship struggles. And (be honest), I would bet that most of you have followed your daily horoscope at some point in your life. In reality, though, Astrology is a complicated subject that involves much more than our zodiac sign or our horoscope. Obviously, this chapter can only provide a cursory overview, and its focus will be on Western Astrology.

What is Astrology?

Astrology is arguably the oldest science in the world. Indeed, for centuries, Astrology formed the foundation of science, medicine, and philosophy. Archaeological records within the ruins of almost every ancient civilization—Greece, Babylon, China, and Rome—reveal that our ancestors relied upon the stars for everything from planting and harvesting to navigation. They not only watched the stars, they tracked other celestial phenomena, such as comets and eclipses, as well as the movement of the sun and moon. Early astrologers noticed that groups of stars seemed to move around the sky together; others, that were much more intense, did not. The distinctive clusters of stars are called constellations, and those brighter stars are known today as planets. Back then, without the benefit of the telescopes of today, our ancestors recognized and named five planets, known as the classical planets: Mercury, Venus, Mars, Jupiter, and Saturn. The planets were named after gods, which is what the ancients believed them to be. Continuing that tradition, modern astronomers, of course, discovered three others, dubbed the modern planets: Uranus, Neptune, and Pluto. Along with our sun, this family of planets makes up our Solar System.

The ancient Babylonians divided the night sky into twelve sections, naming each one after its largest constellation. This zodiac calendar helped them track time, but perhaps more importantly, it enabled them to make predictions. The Babylonians observed correlations between the movement of the planets (called *transits*), and key events in their lives, both favorable and unfavorable. At the dawn of the first century, the roles of the planets and stars formed the basis of elaborate Roman myths. Eventually, it was in the merging of both the folklore and the meticulous observation, that Astronomy was born. Today, we recognize both Astrology, which looks at the relationship between the celestial bodies and our human Selves, and Astronomy, the scientific study of the Solar System.

Not only is Astrology related to Astronomy, some consider Astrology to be the elder sister of Psychology, as both disciplines deal with the psyche and are comprised of various *schools*, based on their approach. In particular, Carl Jung's Analytical Psychology, espouses many concepts that closely parallel those of Astrology, such as the importance of the individual psyche, the personal quest for wholeness, and the idea that humans are born with an innate disposition. It is this innate nature that Astrologers seek to uncover, primarily through the birth chart.

How it Works

Astrologists believe that, in addition to our heredity and our environment, the lives of human beings are also influenced by the state of our solar system at the time of our birth. This solar system snapshot, called a natal horoscope (or birth chart), is calculated using the date, time, and place of birth. The natal horoscope, or *map of the psyche*, can uncover traits and characteristics that haven't yet revealed themselves in our conscious awareness. While our horoscope can't predict the future, it can certainly tell us a lot about our personality, motivations, and desires. Therefore, understanding our birth chart might help us choose a compatible partner, select and train for a rewarding career, or take care of our physical and emotional well-being.

Not unlike a theater production, the astrological chart begins with a few essential pieces: the actors (celestial bodies), their roles (the zodiac signs), and the stage (the houses). A brief description of the characteristics of each of these pieces is provided below. Let's start with the celestial bodies. The Sun, Moon, and planets—the actors—are associated with certain facets of our nature:

Sun: Our goals and desires.

Moon: Our feelings and emotional responses.

Mercury: Our thoughts and expressions.

Venus: How we relate to others.

Mars: How we harness our energy and talent to achieve our goals.

Jupiter: How we pursue joy and understanding.

Saturn: Our self-discipline and strength of character.

Uranus: Our creative nature.

Neptune: How we can best serve others.

Pluto: Our growth through self-knowledge.

Next up, we have the zodiac signs. At birth, the position of the sun is what determines our zodiac sign (also called the *Sun Sign* or *birth sign*). These signs give the planets their *personality*, revealing how we tend to respond to the events of our lives. The twelve zodiac signs can be likened to the roles that are played by the planet-actors:

Aries: (March 21 – April 19) initiative, individuality, action, courage, willpower, impulsivity

Taurus: (April 20 – May 20) values, pleasure, security, income, resolution

Gemini: (May 21 – June 20) communicative, siblings, peers, clever, student

Cancer: (June 21 – July 22) family, financial security, home, emotional base, stubborn

Leo: (July 23 – August 22) creativity, self-expression, ego, romance, generous, dramatic

Virgo: (August 23 – September 22) health, fitness, details, analysis, organization, industrious

Libra: (September 23 – October 22) partnerships, tactful, commitments, harmony and balance

Scorpio: (October 23 – November 21) passion, shared resources, spirituality, transformation, extreme

Sagittarius: (November 22 – December 21) wisdom, travel, global ties, publishing, carefree, sunny

Capricorn: (December 22 – January 19) career, structure, ambitious, public image, proud

Aquarius: (January 20 – February 18) idealism, community, humanitarian, technology, communicative

Pisces: (February 19 – March 20) social, dreams, imagination, illusion, helpful, sensitive, adaptable

Lastly, the planets act out their drama within the twelve houses—their stage. The specific house that a planet is in determines the energy that is brought into that part of our life (career, home, relationships, etc.), as each house represents a different part of life:

First: personality, appearances, first impressions, attitude

Second: money, values, environment, possessions

Third: community, siblings, friends, neighbors,

Fourth: father, family, roots, emotional foundation, youth

Fifth: romance, play, self-expression, creativity

Sixth: health, fitness, organization, service, routine, work

Seventh: relationships, partnerships, sharing

Eighth: bonding, common property, loss, metaphysics

Ninth: travel, study, spirituality, life philosophy

Tenth: occupation, goals, fame and success, achievement, public image, mother

Eleventh: groups, friends, social causes, teachers

Twelfth: endings, healing, closure, spiritual retreats

Although there are a few other components that make up the birth chart, this is a good starting point, since the goal here is to provide a basic understanding of the chart and its purpose. Getting a look at your birth chart is relatively easy. Many websites have a program that will create your birth chart, once you enter your date, time, and place of birth. That being said, if you are truly interested in exploring your chart on more than a superficial level, I would highly recommend having your chart read by a competent Astrologer, in light of its complexity. Due to the way in which each piece (planets, signs, and houses) interacts with every other piece, a deep dive into your chart is best left to a professional. On the other hand, perusing a free birth chart is a fun way to dip your toe into the water, and who knows . . . you might even decide to jump in!

How it Can Help

Thus far, all of the modalities in this section—self-discovery—are designed to turn our focus inward, to find that internal essence of who we are, and Astrology is no different. Although our astrological chart is a very detailed map of who we are both internally (true Self) *and* externally (how Self interacts with the world), it is the birth sign that reveals our inner landscape. So, it is important to start our exploration there, with that internal nugget of Self. And yet, our chart is infinitely more intricate than just a description of our zodiac sign, which is why two Scorpios (like Bill and I) can appear to be quite unique. This is where the many variables within Astrology come into play—nuances that can refine your understanding of Self.

In addition to providing foundational information about Self, a good portion of our birth chart describes the Self in relation to the external world, characteristics and proclivities that might influence how we navigate life's journey—the journey that you began when you picked up this book. The first part of this journey involves rediscovering yourself, while the remaining pieces focus on communicating with Self and healing of Self. With that in mind, starting at the center of your birth chart (true Self) and working your way outward (Self in relationship with the World) will provide you with sufficient self-knowledge to draw in the people and experiences that will fortify your growth. For example, your chart can describe your communication style, methods of self-expression and creativity, and approach to learning. All of those characteristics will guide you to the practices and modalities that work best for you as you continue your journey.

Our ancestors understood that humans are one with the universe and with each other. Studying Astrology, or any of the other modalities in this section, can help us to remember this truth, along with the remembrance of our true nature, our essence. These practices open up the channel to our Higher Selves. Once we embrace the essence of *who we really are* and understand that our HS is connected to *everything* in the universe (through the Quantum Field), we realize that we can use that connection to communicate with the All.

Resources: Part One

Books:

Awake in the World: 108 Practices to Live a Divinely Inspired Life by Debra Moffitt

Conversations with God by Neale Donald Walsch

Making Sense of Scripture: Big Questions about the Book of Faith by David Lose

The Bible Doesn't Say That: 40 Biblical Mistranslations, Misconceptions, and Other Misunderstandings by Joel Hoffman

At Home in the World: Stories and Essential Teachings from a Monk's Life by Thich Nhat Hanh

The Boy Who Knew Too Much: An Astounding True Story of a Young Boy's Past-Life Memories by Cathy Byrd

Life Before Life: A Scientific Investigation of Children's Memories of Previous Lives by Jim Tucker

Many Lives, Many Masters: The True Story of a Prominent Psychiatrist, His Young Patient, and the Past-Life Therapy That Changed Both Their Lives by Brian Weiss

Websites:

Unity Worldwide Ministries: https://www.unity.org/

Agape International Spiritual Center: https://agapelive.com/

Palouse Mindfulness (MBSR) Course:
https://palousemindfulness.com/index.html

Worldwide labyrinth locator: https://labyrinthlocator.com/

The Chopra Center: https://chopra.com/

Learn more about Beyond Quantum Healing (BQH):
https://www.quantumhealers.com/

Learn more about Quantum Healing Hypnosis Technique®
(QHHT): https://dolorescannon.com/

Learn more about Life between Lives®:
https://www.newtoninstitute.org/

Part Two: Communication

"God speaks all the time if we care enough to listen."
Oluwakemi Ola-Ojo

"Carl Gustav Jung asserted that all people share a collective subconscious and, therefore, are able to communicate with each other quite well."
Michael Nir

OK, then. We've finally started to access that part of ourselves we call our true essence, our Higher Self (HS). We are learning to quiet our minds, get rid of distractions, manage our fear, and observe without judgment. Now what? Now that we've opened that channel to our HS, how do we communicate with it? Furthermore, is there anything else we can communicate with? The first section of this book, Self-Discovery, introduced the concept of the Quantum Field (QF). Before we go any further, let's explore this thing called the QF in a little more detail.

Quantum Field

I'd be willing to bet that most of us, somewhere around fifth grade, learned that all matter consists of tiny particles called atoms, which are further divided into protons, neutrons, and electrons. We probably even created some kind of molecule using Styrofoam balls and pipe cleaners, right? Well, scientists now believe that when reduced even further, the tiniest of particles are actually vibrating strings of energy (hence the term, String Theory). As we already know, energy waves carry information (i.e., radio waves). What this means, in layman's terms, is that *everything* in the universe, at its very core, is made up of vibrating waves of information-carrying energy...the book you are holding, the thoughts you are thinking...even YOU. All of this *stuff*, this vibrating energy, is contained in what we call the QF.

Now, can you see these waves of vibrating energy? The answer is . . . sometimes. If the vibration is slow enough, you will be able to perceive it with one or all of your five senses; it will take form and shape, like your coffee table. If the vibration is fast, you will no longer perceive it, just like you can't *see* the energy that powers your microwave, allows for a cellphone call, or produces a picture on the television. In those cases you simply *trust* that the process is happening. You put your food in the microwave, close the door, push a few buttons, and voila, the food is cooked! Did you *see* the energy that cooked your food? My guess is—no. A box fan is another great example of this concept. At very slow speeds, you can see the blades, but once the fan spins fast enough, the individual fan blades can no longer be perceived with your eyes.

Communicating with the QF

What this means for us in terms of communicating with the QF is that because *we* are a part of the QF, we have access to all of the information that is stored within any other part of the QF. What might this look like? Well, has anyone ever spoken something out loud that you were just thinking? Have you ever walked into a room where an argument had just taken place and you could "sense" the negative energy? Do you somehow *know* when a loved one is in trouble and needs help? Have you ever received a phone call from a close friend or relative at the moment you were thinking of them? In those cases, energetic information was being passed from one human to another in a way that bypassed your five senses. The information was conveyed through this QF.

Information within the QF can also be passed along by beings that either no longer exist in our physical realm (i.e., deceased loved ones) or *never* existed in the physical realm (i.e., angels), because *they (still) exist* within the QF! They are energetic beings just like us; they are just vibrating at a much higher rate—too high to be experienced (usually) through our normal senses. These beings reside, for lack of a better word, within what we call the Spirit Realm.

Each and every one of us has a team of beings that works with us throughout our lives. This may not be surprising; most folks are familiar with the concept of guardian angels who watch over us, protecting and guiding us. But there are many, many more! Our spiritual team of helpers could include Ascended Masters or other Biblical figures (like Jesus or Mother Mary), Archangels (the most well-known include Gabriel, Raphael, and Michael), Spirit Animals, or even our deceased family members or pets. The energy of these beings exists within the QF, just like we do; however, their vibration is too fast for most humans to experience with their five senses. That's why we often feel alone and unconnected. We don't realize how much assistance we really have!

What the Bible Says About this Communication

Many Christians believe that communicating with those in the Spirit Realm is prohibited, even demonic. Indeed, there are quite a few Old Testament scriptures that seem to uphold that perspective: "Do not turn to mediums or necromancers; do not seek them out, and so make yourselves unclean by them: I am the Lord your God." (Leviticus 19:31) and "For these nations, which you are about to dispossess, listen to fortune-tellers and to diviners. But as for you, the Lord your God has not allowed you to do this." (Deuteronomy 18:14). There are plenty more, but for the most part, they all say the same thing—don't seek out a medium/fortune-teller/diviner. Another wrinkle within this concept is that some Christians assert that there is no After-life—there is just a temporary "holding pattern" that we enter once we die, where we await our final judgment at the time of the Second Coming of Christ. Then, those who pass muster will be resurrected and will live in a heaven on Earth. Those who don't . . . well, we know where they go.

As it turns out, the passages that warn us against *necromancy* (communicating with the dead) are relegated to the Old Testament, which is important to note because not only does the New Testament *not* prohibit Spirit communication, actually it provides many examples of this and other paranormal activity—levitation, materialization, and mental mediumship among them—very often through Jesus himself. He often spoke of the

Afterlife and that his own followers should expect communication from him after his death. In the Gospel of John, Jesus said, "I will not leave you as orphans; I will come to you. Before long, the world will not see me anymore, but you will see me. Because I live, you also will live." (John 14:18-19).

An extraordinary description of levitation occurs in Matthew 14:22-23, when Jesus and Peter both walked on water (although Peter's experience was cut short due to his doubt). The disciples were spooked at first, thinking that Jesus was a ghost as he walked across the water toward their boat. In a feat of mental mediumship described in Luke 19:28-35, Jesus tells two of his disciples to go ahead of him into the next village; he says that they will find a colt tied up, which they should untie and bring back to him.

A final example, one that is perhaps the most famous account of Spirit communication in the Bible, is The Transfiguration, described in Mark 9:2-9 (as well as Matthew 17:1-3 and Luke 9:28-36). During this miraculous event, Peter, James and John stood mesmerized as Jesus transformed into an ethereal being, Elijah and Moses (who were dead) materialized, and a voice from the clouds (presumably God) boldly addressed them all. In this one event, the three disciples saw Spirit, heard Spirit, and watched Jesus change from human form into Spirit and then back again. There are many more of these mystical experiences described in the New Testament, suggesting that Jesus had no problem violating the rules of the Old Testament. (As an aside, the New Testament contains quite a few instances of Jesus breaking Old Testament law, including Sabbath laws and kosher dietary laws).

So, why is there such a discrepancy between what was written in the Old Testament and the astonishing events described in the New Testament? As I dug deeper, I found that some Bible scholars believe that after 30 AD, in order to maintain control over the masses, the Church simply forbade this type of communication unless it was facilitated by the Church itself. Giving people direct access to the Afterlife would have weakened the Church's power. After all, who needs to listen to the Church (and obey its rules) if you can find out the truth for yourself? Interestingly, this theory not only presumes an Afterlife but that the deceased can be communicated with. The Church just didn't want laypeople doing the communicating! Does that mean that early church leaders influenced the Old Testament? In light of the information presented in Chapter 2, it's not out of the realm of possibility. But perhaps that is a moot point, given what else I found.

In 1953, the Church's Fellowship for Psychical and Spiritual Studies (CFPSS) was founded to promote the study and the integration of psychical and spiritual experience within a Christian context. CFPSS supports what it calls *psychic sensitivity* and believes that theologians should seriously and humbly evaluate all empirical evidence of psychic phenomenon. The Reverend Canon Dr. Michael Perry (deceased), who is ordained in the Church of England, served as the president of CFPSS for many years, as well as the editor of its journal, *The Christian Parapsychologist*. He also served on the Advisory Council of the Academy of Religion and Psychical Research. In 2003, Dr. Perry wrote a book entitled *Psychical and Spiritual* as a tribute to, and in support of, the psychically sensitive.

Perry upholds that the Christian belief that spirit communication is forbidden comes from adhering to an Old Testament understanding of God. In a 2007 interview with Michael Tymn, Perry stated that the writers of the Old Testament were surprisingly uninterested in what happens to us after death. They were primarily concerned with the here and now, which was reflected in their attitude toward their God, Jahweh. They viewed Him as the God of the *living*. Therefore, attempts at psychic communication (contacting the *non-living*) were considered disloyal to God and were prohibited. During this same timeframe, however, their peers—the Tibetan Buddhists and the ancient Egyptians— had a much more robust interest in this type of communication. Perry explains that Jesus's resurrection, which proved that God is the God of both Heaven and Earth, turned the Old Testament beliefs upside down. Even the Roman Catholic Church has acquiesced! After using their own mediums to conduct experiments investigating the practice of Spirit communication, Father Gino Concetti, a prominent Vatican theologian, stated that based on new discoveries in the realm of the paranormal, the Church would no longer forbid a dialogue with the deceased. Perry, the CFPSS, the Vatican, and many other Christians have come to understand that we are not being disloyal to God by contacting the Spirit Realm, particularly if such communication serves to strengthen our own relationship with God.

How this Communication Can Be Helpful

Now that we have established that neither the Church nor Jesus himself take issue with spirit communication you might be wondering *why* we would seek out this type of communication. First, it is important to remember that when we access information from the Quantum Field (QF), we are not just accessing our spiritual team members and ancestors (the Spirit Realm). We have access, through our Higher Self, to ALL information that is stored in the QF. And we call it *communication* because we can ask questions and receive answers. It is a back-and-forth process. Once we become adept at this process, we can tap into this vast pool of knowledge on a daily basis, using it to guide our lives and fulfill our purpose. This is what is meant by using our *intuition*. Your intuition is the way that your HS speaks *to* you and *through* you. When we are tapped into the QF through an alignment with our HS, the circumstances of our lives start to fall in place. People and experiences show up *coincidentally*. We receive inspiration. Things begin to make sense. And this is where life gets exciting!

The Clair-s

As I mentioned earlier, information from the QF is typically not accessible through our five primary senses (sight, hearing, smell, taste and touch) because the information exists in an energetic, rather than physical, state. Not to worry! Even though we may not realize it, human beings come equipped with four alternative senses that allow us to tap into this energetic field. These senses are commonly called the Four Clair-s:

Clairvoyance (clear seeing) – the ability to perceive images or visual impressions within the mind.

Clairaudience (clear hearing) – the ability to hear messages that manifest audibly, typically telepathically.

Clairsentience (clear feeling) – the ability to feel messages or energy within the body.

Claircognizance (clear knowing) – the ability to *just know* the information.

Remember when I received a *knowing* from God that I was to start a healing team in my church? I didn't understand it then, but that was an example of claircognizance. Although we have the ability to receive information through any of these avenues, usually one or two of them will be dominant. For me, information typically comes as a knowing, but I do experience clairvoyance, on occasion. By the way, James Van Praagh, a well-known evidential medium, has a fun quiz on his website that can help you determine which *clair* is your strongest.

Sometimes information comes to us *spontaneously*, while engaging in the normal activities of life. We might recognize this as a spark of inspiration or an *Aha!* moment. This type of information comes during our dream state, as well. However, dreams can be difficult to remember or make sense of. Keeping a dream journal can be beneficial because it helps us identify patterns and discover the meaning of the various symbols we encounter in our dreams. Not only does information come to us spontaneously, we can also receive this information *intentionally* by seeking it out. For instance, as we become practiced meditators, we can set an intention to receive clarity on a particular question or issue. We can also utilize intention-setting prior to bedtime and allow our HS to work as we sleep! But, perhaps the best way to hone your ability to intentionally communicate with the QF is by practicing with and refining your *clair-s*.

Communication through Signs

We've already established that *most* of the time, information from the QF is not accessible through our five primary senses. There are times, though, when folks receive messages through normal sensory experiences—physical signs—very often from an ancestor or spiritual team member. I want to take a moment to talk about those types of signs because not only are they fairly common, they also qualify as communication . . . that is, as long as the receiver *gets* the message!

In my own experience, I often receive messages from my spiritual team through a song on the radio. It might be a specific lyric that I'm drawn to or perhaps just the song title. When this happens, it's usually in response to something I was just thinking about. The messages that pop in simply remind me that those in spirit are aware of what's going on in my life. It's like they are saying, *Hey, we're thinking of you!* or, *We've got your back!* These messages reassure me and remind me that I'm never alone.

People also report finding physical signs, such as a coin, feather, butterfly, bird, or some other object that is associated with a loved one in spirit. We might even see signs in the clouds, like a student I worked with whose deceased mother connected with him in that way. Those who are particularly sensitive might actually feel a touch, perhaps a stroke on the cheek, for example. The deceased father of a girlfriend of mine will sound her wind chimes, even when the air is completely still, in response to her thoughts of him. She finds this very comforting. I have even read of people finding handprints on the bathroom mirror or indentations on the couch, seeing lights flicker on and off, smelling the perfume of a loved one, and hearing unexplained music.

Through the examples above, we can see that this kind of communication takes place in all sorts of ways. Your spiritual team will attempt to communicate with you in the easiest way possible and in a way that you will be most open to. For example, if you prefer instrumental music, your team probably won't try to communicate through song lyrics. However, if you are a gardener, you might receive signs by way of the flowers, birds, or other critters. The truth is, we *can* communicate with things that are outside of our physical *reality*. We just have to create the space and pay attention, which you can do by practicing the suggestions in the first section of this book.

The next few chapters will highlight some common methods for setting up an intentional line of communication between you (your Higher Self) and the Quantum Field.

Chapter 8 - Numerology

Numerology—the science of names and numbers—was birthed from the idea that the very fabric of the universe can be reduced to a system of numbers. This concept is, in fact, scientifically valid. MIT cosmologist Max Tegmark, author of *Our Mathematical Universe: My Quest for the Ultimate Nature of Reality*, believes that *everything*, living and nonliving, is part of a mathematical configuration. Even space, that illusory substance in which everything else exists, can ultimately be described as a mathematical structure. Tegmark goes so far as to suggest that math will one day be able to explain consciousness itself! This is exciting, as it assumes a compatible relationship between science and spirituality; the two fields don't have to be mutually exclusive.

If the universe is indeed based on a system of numbers, it would follow then that we can use those numbers to better understand ourselves and our world. Like Astrology, Numerology can help us discover insights about our purpose and personality traits, compatible partners, and fulfilling career paths. For that reason, Numerology could just as easily have been included in part one, Self-discovery. As a modality, Numerology has multiple uses. In fact, I would highly recommend that you play with that side of it; the self-discovery aspect is fascinating. But watch out—it can be addictive. You'll probably want to compute the Life Path number for everyone you know. All of that aside, Numerology, considered to be a universal language of numbers, can also be used as a form of communication between you and the QF, and that will be the focus of this chapter.

What is Numerology?

The earliest written records of Numerology were found in ancient Egypt and Babylon roughly 4,000-5,000 years ago. It was also around this time that the Hebrews developed a number system called the Chaldean system, considered to be the oldest form of Numerology. In addition, there is evidence that similar number systems were used in ancient China, Rome, Japan, and Greece, as well. During the sixth century BC, Pythagoras, a well-respected Greek mathematician and philosopher, formed the foundation for what would eventually become modern-day Numerology. Pythagoras taught mathematics, astronomy, and music, and if his name sounds familiar, it is probably because you learned his theorems in your high school Geometry course (not one of my favorites, to be honest). Like our current scientists, he also believed that the entire universe could be expressed through numbers. He eventually developed his own system of numbers that was later expanded upon by other Greek philosophers. Dr. Julian Stenton is typically credited with bringing this metaphysical science into common practice and calling it Numerology. Although it is gaining in popularity, Numerology is not one of the most well-known metaphysical practices.

Pythagorus, as a philosopher, believed that numbers held significance not only scientifically but spiritually, as well. Indeed, throughout history, religion, and mythology, numbers have held a special meaning. As a Christian, I was aware of many spiritually significant numbers. For example, the number three is all over the Bible, 467 times in fact. It represents the trinity and the resurrection, for starters. At 735 mentions, the number seven appears even more frequently, and if we include the words "sevenfold" or "seventh," the number of references jumps to 860. Seven is often associated with God's creative abilities and endeavors. Even in the secular world, we understand, if only superficially, that there is some inherent meaning behind numbers. After all, bad news comes in threes, right? (Celebrity deaths do too, I've heard.) But the question remains…why have we held so tightly, over *thousands* of years, to this idea that numbers are significant . . . that they play some sort of important role in our lives? Could there really be something to it?

How it Works

In the most common form of Numerology today, called Pythagorean Numerology, each letter of the alphabet is assigned a number from 1-9 (the Chaldean system used only the numbers 1-8). This design allows for numeric calculations based on your birth name; your *destiny* and *personality* numbers are calculated using your birth name. Along with the *destiny* and *personality* numbers, your *life path* number—derived by adding up the numbers in your full date of birth—can provide you with a great deal of personal insight, similar in detail to an Astrological chart. There are many free online programs that will calculate those numbers for you (or explain how . . . it's not difficult), as well as provide some level of information about what your numbers mean. Again, though, for a more in-depth reading that is both thorough and accurate, I would suggest visiting a competent Numerologist. That said, exploring the free sites or reading a book about Numerology (I started with a great one by Glynis McCants) can be a fun way to play with this modality and see if it resonates.

As we've learned, Numerology is a modality that can provide a plethora of insight about not only our personal Self but how we interact with the world. However, there is also another way that we can use numbers to interact with the world—the world of Spirit, that is, or what we've been calling the QF. Earlier, I explained that everything in the universe can be reduced to tiny, information-filled strings of energy, all vibrating at a particular frequency. Numbers are no different; each and every number holds a particular vibration. And because all of this energy is connected through the QF, it can (and does) communicate. This means that numbers can also communicate with us and provide us with information. This often happens in one of two ways: either the numbers themselves hold a meaning for us, one that we may understand on a conscious or subconscious level, or other beings in the QF, perhaps an ancestor or guardian angel, will use those numbers to get our attention.

Have you ever wondered why you frequently see certain numbers or number combinations? In my life, it started with 1, 2, 3, 4. I'd see those numbers on the clock *all the time*! It then progressed to repetitive numbers such as 1111, 4444, and so on. In fact, on my way to my very first Reiki training, I got behind a car whose license plate was all 1s.

Although I had no idea what any of this meant or if it meant anything at all, I got excited about it. I felt like I was noticing those numbers on purpose, as if something (or someone?) was trying to get my attention. So, I started paying attention to what was going on at the exact time that I noticed the number combinations. What was playing on the radio? Who was it that called me at 11:11? What did they say? What was I dreaming about when I woke up at 4:44 a.m.? It was through numbers that I was opened up to the idea of *synchronicity*.

Seeing repetitive numbers is a form of synchronicity. Carl Jung described the phenomena of synchronicity as a meaningful coincidence that couldn't have been due to chance alone. My Texas pastor used to call coincidences "God-instances," and I think he's right. To me, there's no doubt that within the QF, everything weaves itself into a beautiful tapestry or web of creation. Synchronicity is simply our recognition of the web's existence. In that moment, the connection between our HS and the QF opens up, providing us with a message or a piece of information.

There are some really good books and websites that describe the meaning behind hundreds of numbers, but it is also important to determine what the numbers mean to you personally. Not unlike trying to uncover the meaning of a dream in a dream book, symbols are highly personal and not every symbol will mean the same thing to all people.

For instance, in a dream, a bear might represent something fearful to me, but to someone whose animal guide is a bear, it might bring comfort. The same thing holds true for numbers. Nevertheless, here are some common meanings behind the numbers 0-9:

0 – All about God and God's love.

1 – Powerful number for manifesting; keep your mind on what you wish to create.

2 – Keep the faith; believe; everything is going to be ok.

3 – An ascended master is working with you or has a message for you.

4 – The most famous number, angels are with you.

5 – All about change; a significant change is coming into your life.

6 – Represents the material things in your life; may indicate a sense of worry.

7 – You are on the right path; things are going well, probably better than you imagine.

8 – Abundance and prosperity.

9 – Pushes you to get busy with life's purpose; do something/anything, stop procrastinating.

How it Can Help

Understanding the meaning of numbers will not only give you that extra bit of personal insight, it can also open the door of communication between you and the QF. As I mentioned in the introduction to this section, your spiritual team will attempt to communicate with you in the way that you will best understand; messages will take the easiest path.

Here's a great example: I recently met a young woman who attended a group event I facilitated at a local spiritual co-op. As I was packing up, she approached me to relate a series of "crazy" things she had been experiencing lately. "For instance," she said, "I keep seeing all of these numbers . . . repetitive number sequences . . . they're everywhere!" She went on to explain that she didn't know what to make of all this metaphysical stuff, as she worked in IT—a typical left-brained occupation. Do you see the beauty in this? Her team was speaking to her in numbers! They knew it was a language that she would understand.

Perhaps seeing a repetitive number will simply confirm that you are on the right track, like it did for me when I was driving to my Reiki training. Or you might ask for number signs from your spiritual team when you are first learning how to communicate with them. When faced with a decision, you can even request a sign to help you choose the best option. Often times, numbers are simply an entry point, the gateway into an understanding that there is more to our world than meets the eye—an understanding that we are more than just our physical bodies. Once they have our attention, there is no end to the ways in which our team members can communicate with us.

By the way, the number fourteen (in the title of this book) *inspires change, renewal, and growth* and encourages us to *share our knowledge and wisdom with others.* Interestingly, I had settled on the number fourteen very early in the book's planning stages, long before looking up its meaning. And, if that's not coincidental enough, here's yet another example of how the universe communicates through numbers: As I was conducting a final proof of this manuscript—this creative work that I had just birthed—I got to the part about numbers in Christianity, and my eyes landed (again) on the following sentence: *Seven is often associated with God's creative abilities and endeavors.* Did I mention that my Life Path number is seven? (Not surprisingly, *sevens* are also spiritual seekers, who are quite intuitive and trust their internal guidance system). Hmmm . . .

Keep reading to discover even more communication methods!

Chapter 9 - Tarot and Oracle Cards

Shortly after my first Reiki training, I decided to purchase a deck of oracle cards. I had already stepped *way* outside my comfort zone by attending the Reiki class, so I was feeling rather emboldened. I had learned a little bit about oracle cards during my Reiki training (discussed in greater detail in chapter 14), but I wasn't drawn to traditional tarot cards, as they were still a bit intimidating to me at that point. An ordinary deck of oracle cards seemed like a relatively harmless way to seek guidance from...well, I wasn't sure yet . . . God? My guardian angels? Either way, this would be my first *deliberate* attempt at communication. I headed to Barnes & Noble, because I wanted to see the decks up close and in person, rather than purchase one from an online retailer. I quickly located the appropriate bookshelf and immediately had two thoughts, 1) *Good grief, I had no idea there were so many decks of cards to choose from!* and, as I furtively looked around, 2) *I sure hope I don't run into anyone I know!* After all, although I was exploring new territory, I had not yet *come out* to my friends or extended family and wasn't ready to explain how I wound up on this aisle.

After perusing the various decks, I settled on one called The Soul's Journey Lesson Cards by James Van Praagh (JVP), a well-known medium who I had seen on the Oprah Winfrey show. If he's safe enough for Oprah, I thought, he must be OK! Besides, *lesson cards* sounded much more benign than tarot cards. As I approached the counter to pay, eyes still darting back and forth to avoid being spotted with this questionable merchandise, something behind the register caught my eye. There, on a shelf just behind the cashier's left shoulder sat a big, red heart. It was a paperweight, lying in an open gift box, staring right at me. I'm curiously drawn to hearts, so I instinctively knew this was a sign that I was on the right path. Turns out, I was right; they were the perfect cards for a newbie, and I still use them frequently. Since then, I've purchased a few more decks, and I alternate between them depending on the circumstance.

What is Tarot?

The Tarot is arguably one of the most popular and well-known instruments of divination in the world. Originally created as a parlor game, tarot cards started to appear in France and Italy during the late fourteenth century. European artists crafted those early decks, which contained four suits: staves (or *wands*), discs (also called *pentacles* or *coins*), cups, and swords. During the mid-fifteenth century, the trump (or triumph) cards were added, and wealthy families would commission artists to hand paint personalized decks. Until the printing press was invented, which allowed cards to be mass-produced, the cards were not available to the average citizen. By the late sixteenth and early seventeenth centuries, tarot cards had gained in popularity as a loosely-based divination tool. By the eighteenth century, the Tarot was being used in a more structured manner, with unique *spreads* and specific card meanings.

In the late 1700s, a theory emerged that the symbolism in the Tarot was originally derived from the ancient esoteric knowledge of Egyptian priests, had subsequently found its way to the popes and the Roman Catholic Church, and was now being suppressed. Although there was never any historical documentation to uphold this theory, it nevertheless caused resurgence in the interest of tarot and its link to the occult. In 1791, a French occultist by the name of Jean-Baptiste Alliette created the first tarot deck specifically designed for divination rather than entertainment. In 1909, Arthur Waite, a British occultist, and artist Pamela Colman Smith created the iconic Rider-Waite Tarot deck (sometimes referred to as the Waite-Smith deck), which is still used widely today and is often the default deck in tarot instruction manuals.

How it Works

The traditional, Rider-Waite deck is comprised of seventy-eight cards. Twenty-two of those cards make up the *Major Arcana*, with symbolism pertaining to the material world, the intuitive mind, and the realm of change. The remaining fifty-six cards make up the *Minor Arcana*, and they are divided into four suits that are focused on specific themes: *Swords* indicate conflict or moral issues; *Pentacles* represent the material aspects of life;

Wands deal with jobs and ambition; and *Cups* involve relationships and emotions. Cards are laid out in spreads, or layouts, depending on the preference of the reader or the needs of the client. Spreads can be as simple as pulling one card, used for daily guidance, for example, or a three-card spread that represents the client's past, present, and future. The most well-known layout is the ten-card Celtic Cross method, but other popular spreads include the ten-card Tree of Life and the twenty-one-card Romany. There are even spreads that focus on specific issues, like career, romance, and relationships, and those that are done at certain times, such as during a new or full moon.

We've talked a lot about tarot cards, but what about oracle cards? Sometimes, those words, tarot and oracle, are used interchangeably, but are they really the same thing? Well, almost. Any card deck can be considered an oracle deck if it is used to access intuitive information; therefore, all tarot cards can be called oracle cards. However, not all oracle cards can be defined as tarot, because tarot cards must meet certain criteria. For example, while traditional tarot decks have seventy-eight cards, oracle card decks can contain as few as twelve cards or as many as a hundred. In addition, while the images might vary within tarot decks, the messaging is typically consistent, with cards that hold the same symbolic meanings. One other difference between the two is that oracle cards tend to provide a more generalized sense of what's happening, while tarot cards offer more detailed interpretations. This is because traditional tarot primarily uses a multi-card spread, while oracle cards are often pulled one at a time.

While it is true that anyone can learn how to read tarot, most practitioners view tarot as an art; that is to say, a reading is, in essence, a unique blend of knowledge and intuition. In this way, we acknowledge the card deck as a tool with which we can access the QF. As we learn about the cards and the process, however, we discover that card reading is a lot like a language. Becoming adept at deciphering the language strengthens the information we receive, both in detail and clarity. So, while it is important to learn the meaning behind each card, it is equally important to use your intuition to guide the reading. With this in mind, it is a good idea to select a card deck that you feel comfortable with, perhaps one to which you feel intuitively drawn. It may even be that you select several decks to use in different situations. Rare is the practitioner who owns only one deck.

Due to its popularity, and perhaps because traditional tarot can be off-putting, unique oracle card decks have been created for folks from all walks of life and all levels of experience. If your head was spinning at the number of yoga classes available, wait until you start searching for your first card deck. There are cards that focus on Ascended Masters, Saints, and Archangels; decks having to do with flowers, trees, and water; cards for dog, cat, rabbit, unicorn, dolphin, and horse lovers; and even decks for those into Star Wars, crop circles, and extraterrestrials.

Oracle cards (as opposed to traditional tarot cards) come in a wide range of styles and topics, so they tend to be much easier to pick up and use right out of the box. There is usually a small manual that comes with the deck, as well, that explains how to use them and the meaning of each card. Some cards might offer a positive affirmation for the day (check out Louise Hay's decks), an inspiring message (Gabrielle Bernstein) or perhaps a quote from a popular philosophical concept, like manifesting (Abraham-Hicks) or past lives (Brian Weiss).

How it Can Help

As I discovered early on in my exploration, oracle cards are an easy way to start listening to that subtle whisper from the Spirit Realm. They offer a simple, straightforward tool to help us connect with the QF, particularly when we are just beginning the journey and our connection is weak. At first, I would pull a card from my JVP deck each day, and I was flabbergasted at how accurately the card related to something that was going on in my life. If I were dealing with a worrisome issue and needed advice, I'd pull a card, and again, the card was spot on. Receiving affirmation from my cards confirmed to me that I really did have a spiritual team and I actually could hear from them. Over time, I gravitated to other decks that could be used in specific circumstances. For example, Radleigh Valentine's *Angel Answers Oracle Cards* are great if I want a more concrete answer to a decision I need to make, and his *Angel Tarot Cards* work well for general guidance. Sometimes, I'll even pull a card from two different decks, giving me two perspectives from which to view a situation.

Because your spiritual team wants to communicate with you, too, oracle cards are a great way to let them know that you are open and listening. Once you start to receive confirmation, your level of trust will skyrocket. Then, it becomes easier to recognize the messages that come forth in other ways. Although I'm no longer dependent on my daily card readings to access information from the QF, I still use them quite often and have a particular fondness for my JVP deck, which helped me to fling open the door to the Spirit Realm.

Chapter 10 - Psychics and Mediums

You've probably heard of someone described as a Psychic Medium, particularly given the prolific number of them on television these days. But what exactly does that mean? This designation—psychic medium—can be misleading, because it actually describes two slightly different abilities. While all mediums are psychic, a person with psychic ability is not always a medium. Both psychics and mediums conduct what is called a *reading*, the relaying of information, for a *sitter*, the person who receives the reading. Psychics are able to tune into the energy of people or objects in order to gather information about a client's past, present, or future. A medium, however, takes the reading a step further, by tuning into the non-physical, or Spirit energy that surrounds the sitter. In other words, a psychic receives information from the sitter's own energy field, while a medium gathers information from the Spirit Realm.

Interestingly, I've learned a lot about this subject over the past few years because my husband Bill discovered, as an adult, that he is a psychic medium. And, if there is one thing I know for sure (as Oprah liked to say), it is that a mediumship reading can be profoundly healing, even life changing, for someone who has lost a loved one. In my experience, evidential mediums—those who provide undeniable evidence of their connection with a loved one in Spirit—act in Divine service to both the physical and spiritual worlds.

What is a Psychic Medium?

Attempting to contact spirits has long been a part of human history; most every culture contains its own version of a medium who could communicate with the deceased. In fact, these oracles were typically revered for their ability to predict natural disasters, crop failures, and other significant events. The earliest instance of mediumship, recorded in a drawing known as the sorcerer, was located in a cave in France and dates back to 13,000 BC. It depicts a man, clothed in deer skin and antlers, who is believed to be channeling the God of Hunting, performing a ritual that would promise success to the upcoming hunt. In ancient Greece and Egypt, mediums played a prominent role in society and were often advisers to royalty and other powerful people. Greek oracles were known to fall into trance states and begin speaking with Spirits, evidenced by the change in their voice and personality. In the sixteenth century, a group known as the Tremblers of Cevennes were recognized for healing the sick by entering a trance state and speaking in tongues. Indeed, spiritual contact, ancestral worship, and soul reverence—precursors to mediumship—can be found in most every major religion, including Christianity.

More recently, however, it wasn't until the birth of Spiritual-ism in the 1850s that mediumship became widely accepted and wildly popular. Spiritualists believe in the ability to communicate with discarnate humans by way of mediums, whom they believe have been blessed with this gift. Although Spiritualism (at that time) was not necessarily viewed as a distinct religious move-ment, it provided those of faith with an explanation for life after death and evidence for the existence of the soul, something their religious leaders were not able to provide. Spiritualists were quite progressive for their time, given the prominent role that both women and laypersons held within the organization. The Society for Psychical Research was established in 1882, tasked with investigating paranormal activity through methods that were rigorous and fair-minded.

And in 1920, the Anglican Communion, one of the world's largest Christian communities, admitted that the Spiritualist movement had provided spiritual meaning and purpose to human life. From the mid-1800s through the mid-1900s, notable figures like Arthur Conan Doyle and Andrew Jackson Davis provided credibility to the practice of mediumship. Séances were extremely popular, being held in royal palaces, the White House, and in other respectable locations. However, as time went on, perhaps because of the number of frauds who falsely claimed these abilities, the practice of mediumship fell into disrepute for many decades.

Today, psychics and mediums are enjoying another wave of popularity, thanks in part to their exposure on cable television. Shows like *The Long Island Medium*, *Hollywood Medium*, and *Psychic Kids* are helping to make mediumship much more mainstream. One of the people attempting to bring this field into the realm of credible science is University of Arizona professor, Dr. Gary Schwartz, director of the Laboratory for Advances in Consciousness and Health. Dr. Schwartz received his Ph.D. from Harvard University, where he subsequently served as an assistant professor for five years, later moving to Yale University, where he served as a professor of psychology and psychiatry. Along with the help of evidence-based mediums and state-of-the-art technology, Dr. Schwartz aims to gain clarity on the existence of the human soul and the survival of consciousness after our physical death.

How it Works

Mediumship is generally divided into two forms: *physical* mediumship and *mental* mediumship. While both require a connection with a being in Spirit, physical mediumship produces some type of outward *communication* that is recognizable to all participants. *Levitation* (the movement of objects without a normal means of support), *materialization* (the full or partial appearance of a being in Spirit), and *automatic writing* (written material provided by Spirit and channeled through the medium) are types of physical mediumship. *Trance* mediumship (also called trance channeling), whereby Spirit communicates through the medium's own voice, often falls into this physical mediumship category, as well. Physical mediumship arguably peaked during the Spiritualist movement of the late eighteenth and early nineteenth centuries, when folks like William Stanton Moses and the Fox sisters would demonstrate these amazing phenomena, particularly during séances. However, channeled or inspired writing is still a popular form of physical mediumship—the works of Neale Donald Walsch and Paul Selig are good examples—as is trance channeling, which can be seen in the work of Lee Carroll, Darryl Anka, and Esther Hicks.

In mental mediumship, communication from Spirit is relayed through the medium, who in turn, verbally relates that information to the sitter. This process is sometimes called telepathic mediumship, since messages often manifest within the medium's mind or *third-eye*. Mediums can receive information from Spirit via any or all of the *clair-s*, described earlier in this section. For example, the medium may feel a physical sensation in their body as a way for the Spirit being to describe the cause of death. Other times, an odor might be presented that is associated with the deceased, such as a particular perfume or flower that they enjoyed, or perhaps the smoke of a cigarette, pipe, or cigar.

Because Spirit beings often *speak* in pictures or symbols, mediums often spend many years honing their craft in order to become proficient at translating the symbols into meaningful messages. Friend and medium Priscilla Keresey (who wrote a lovely endorsement for this book) shared a few of those symbols with me. For her, a wrapped gift represents a birthday. If Spirit pushes the gift toward her, it means that the birthday is coming up soon; if Spirit lifts the gift toward her, it means that Spirit passed before a birthday; and when the gift is presented with a feeling of sadness, Spirit is trying to say that they passed right around someone else's birthday. Two wrapped gifts shown at the same time represent twins or birthdays within a day or two of each other.

As you can see, there are many nuances in Spirit communication that must be learned in order to give a client the evidence that will result in a successful reading. Priscilla also explained that, in the same way one might learn a foreign language, as the medium becomes more proficient in the language of Spirit, they rely less and less on the symbols and more on an overall sense of *knowing*.

A mediumship session can take place in a group setting, often called a mediumship circle, or as an individual reading. In a circle, the medium will typically stand in the middle of a group of about ten to twelve people and attempt to *bring in* the Spirits who wish to communicate with those in attendance. Attendees can claim the information, if it resonates, with a *yes* or *no*, but are usually encouraged not to give more information than that, as it is up to the medium to provide evidence of Spirit connection.

Mediumship circles are a fun way to test the waters, particularly for first-timers or skeptics, although keep in mind, a medium cannot guarantee that everyone in attendance will receive a message. Even in the case of an individual reading, for various reasons, sometimes the Spirit we hope to connect with simply can't or won't come through. Another thing to keep in mind is that, very often, clients can't make an immediate connection to the evidence that is provided. Perhaps the ancestor is not well-known to the client or the client simply doesn't remember. In those cases, it can appear as though the medium is off base, only to discover later, after consulting with other family members, that the medium was spot on. The price for an individual reading can vary greatly; some well-known mediums have long waitlists, even while charging hundreds of dollars. Word of mouth is probably the best way to select a reputable medium, with average prices ranging from $85-$200 per hour.

How it Can Help

Humans today seem ever more anxious, depressed, and hopeless. Thanks to immediate and relentless media coverage, the stress of world crises and natural disasters threaten to overwhelm us. Folks like Gary Schwartz believe that there is only one true solution: the understanding of ourselves as energetic beings who are interconnected within the Quantum Field. Schwartz maintains that this knowledge could eventually lead to global wellness, peace, and abundance. Therefore, according to

Schwartz, it is critically important to shed light on the (heretofore) controversial topic of consciousness and life after death. All too often, though, at least in the most recent past, it has been frowned upon—called unscientific, irrational—to place our trust in psychics or mediums. For those who have lost a loved one, however, Spirit communication can not only mend a broken heart, it can also alleviate our own fear of aging and death.

Ethical, evidential mediums help us understand that love never dies. They reassure us that the deceased are still alive and are now free from pain and suffering. They encourage us to go on living, comforted by the knowledge that they still see us and participate in our day to day existence. Perhaps best of all, though, psychics and mediums can teach us that we, too, can learn to communicate with the Spirit Realm, because our very essence is Spirit. And, when we all grasp the eternal Truth of who we really are, we will experience Heaven on Earth.

Chapter 11 - Angels

As a practicing Christian, I had no problem with angels. In fact, they play a prominent role in religious history—angels are referenced in the Bible almost three hundred times. I knew that angels had communicated with humans in the past, typically heralding critical information. Arguably, one of the most significant angelic messages provided the very foundation for Christianity, when Gabriel told Mary that she would give birth to Jesus, the Son of God. There are even instances today when ordinary folks claim to have encountered an angel; for example, being rescued and comforted by a *stranger* after a traffic accident, only to find that the stranger later disappeared into thin air. But, if you had asked me a few years ago if humans could have ongoing communication with the angelic realm, I would probably have said no. The types of miracles that occurred during biblical times certainly didn't occur nowadays...did they? After all, weren't those ancient people more deserving? Closer to God somehow? Fortunately, I've since learned that God has never stopped communicating with us, and He uses all sorts of messengers, including angels.

What are Angels?

This seems like a silly question, given that almost every culture, whether religious or secular, is saturated with angelic symbolism. We name children and cities after angels, we write movies and songs about them, we light candles and pray to them, we collect all sorts of angelic charms and tchotchkes…there is no limit to the lengths we will go to demonstrate our affinity for these beings. Truly, humans have been in relationship with angels since the dawn of time; they have served as the messengers between mortals and the Divine, spiritual liaisons, if you will. The Greek word *angelos* actually means messenger.

The oldest altar dedicated to angels was found in Iraq, ancient Sumeria, dating back to 3000 BC. But the belief in this type of radiant messenger actually predates the concept of a monotheistic God. For example, ancient Egyptians worshiped the winged deity Isis, while the Greek god Hermes and the Roman god Mercury, both winged, were considered to be swift messengers. In spite of the number of historical references to angels and other winged messengers, there was a surprising lack of agreement about the definition, characteristics, or purpose of angels. There is evidence, for example, that Jesus himself was once thought to be angelic; however, a group of bishops later decided, during the Council of Nicaea in 325, that this was not the case. Some monks of that time believed that only the most moral individuals (like themselves) were granted a guardian angel. Angels were thought to be both creators and destroyers, messengers of joyful events and harbingers of death.

Although not a part of official church doctrine, during the late fourth century AD, the Christian Church grouped angels into three subsets, creating a kind of hierarchy: Seraphim, Cherubim, and Thrones; Dominions, Virtues, and Powers; and Principalities, Archangels, and (Guardian) Angels. This last group of angels—those of the seventh, eighth, and ninth ranking order—are primarily tasked with carrying out Divine tasks on earth and communicating with her inhabitants.

While the Church was busy ranking and organizing the angels, European artists began to depict angels with wings, and during the second half of the Middle Ages, the fascination surrounding angels increased exponentially. The thirteenth century theologian, Thomas Aquinas, wrote a lot about their nature and activities, considering them to be intellectual but purely spiritual beings. Many famous art works were created during this time period, including Michelangelo's marble sculpture, *Angel*, which still stands at the Basilica of San Domenico in Bologna.

Depending upon the poll, roughly three-quarters of Americans today believe in angels, fifty-five percent of whom suggest that guardian angels have protected them in some way. Given those numbers, I think it's safe to say that angels have ingrained themselves in our hearts and minds, but how we can strengthen our personal relationship with them?

How they Work

A better question might be: *How does angel communication work?* Well, very often angels communicate to us through the signs that were described in the introduction to this section on Communication. Of those signs, some are more common when angels are involved, like feathers, coins, and number sequences. Angels may appear in dreams or clouds, as an orb in a photograph, or as lights or sparkles in your periphery—a phenomenon my own angel team used to get my attention recently.

One evening last week, while chatting with some friends, I kept seeing a twinkle of light out of the corner of my left eye. My friends were amused, as I swung my head around and darted my eyes to the side, trying to figure out what I was seeing. I thought it might be a reflection from a strand of fairy hair I had gotten during a local holistic festival (tinsel-like material that gets tied onto a strand of hair). My friends insisted it wasn't; the strand of tinsel was hidden behind my ear.

The interesting thing is that I had already received a verbal message from my intuitive friend, Deb, informing me that I would be working with the angelic realm very soon. Deb was not aware that I was, in fact, preparing to write this chapter on angels. That being said, I still didn't realize that the sparkles were related to my angel team. The next day, while conducting research for this chapter, my eyes widened in surprise as I read the following: *seeing sparkles or flashes of light can mean that angels are near!* I thanked my angelic team for their messages of assurance and asked them for their guidance as I began to write *their* chapter.

Not only will you recognize angels through the signs they provide, they can also present themselves through the four *clair-s* that were mentioned earlier. For instance, you might *see* an angelic vision with your eyes or within your third-eye (clairvoyance), *hear* sweet, angelic music (clairaudience), *feel* a tingling on the top of your head (clairsentience), or simply have an inner *knowing* that angels are near (claircognizance). Sometimes, there is a sweet smell that arises when angels are present or even a change in temperature. People have also described a feeling of warmth or a pleasant vibration deep inside their body. Those who are particularly intuitive might receive information *downloads*, telepathically delivered blocks of thought. This usually happens when a complex idea needs to be conveyed quickly and thoroughly. It may come with pictures, words, or symbols, but it will convey a complete concept. Finally, although angels have never incarnated as a human being (with the exception of Archangels Metatron and Sandalphon), they are able to appear to us in human form if necessary.

Remember, though . . . communication is a two-way street. We've discussed the ways in which angels might *speak* to you, but there are also ways in which you can communicate with them. Deliberate communication requires that we maintain a state of *relaxed receptivity*, which can take some practice. Meditation is a great way to exercise that muscle and designating a consistent time and place to connect each day will make it easier to establish a lasting relationship with your angels. It is also important to approach the angelic realm (or any part of the Spirit realm) from a place of pure intention and to *believe* that you will receive guidance. After that, it is simply a matter of paying attention. Listen to and trust your intuition—the small voice that emanates from the heart, not the head. Be on the lookout for those signs and synchronicities, and when they appear, *give thanks*. Once you sense and acknowledge their presence, your life will be full of angelic guidance.

The remainder of this chapter will focus on the *archangels*, the leaders of the angelic realm. Indeed, the word *archangel* comes from a Greek word meaning *chief angel*. The name of each archangel holds a special meaning that serves to describe its unique mission. Except for Metatron and Sandalphon, spoken about earlier, each name ends in *-el*, meaning *of God*. Although the archangels are charged with communicating and interacting with the human race, they will not intervene in our lives unless we have given them permission; on Earth, free will is considered sacred. The exact number of archangels is unknown. The Anglican tradition references four, arguably the most well-known— Gabriel, Michael, Raphael, and Uriel—while other faiths claim that there are seven. For the purposes of this chapter, I am including fifteen, those that bestselling Hay House author and angel communicator, Radleigh Valentine, believes are the most prominent and powerful.

How they Can Help

Each archangel is associated with a particular color, crystal or gemstone, and a corresponding astrological sign (although, some archangels oversee all of the signs). These characteristics provide us with a rich array of possibilities when working with the archangels. For instance, Raphael, the angel of healing, is associated with the color green and the gemstones emerald and malachite, and he oversees all astrological signs. (Archangels don't really have a gender, but their energy can sometimes feel masculine or feminine.) So, if we need healing, we can call upon Raphael, visualize ourselves being surrounded and infused by soft green light, and even meditate while holding an emerald or piece of malachite. In other words, all of Raphael's attributes can be used to strengthen and enhance our relationship with him. Below, is a description of the primary characteristics of each of the archangels.

Ariel (*Lioness of God*) is the protector and guardian of nature and the environment. She also works closely with Raphael to help in healing, particularly with regard to animals. **Color**: pale pink; **Crystal/Gemstone**: rose quartz; **Astrological sign**: Aries

Azrael (*Angel of God*) comforts those who are grieving and supports grief counselors. He also guides souls to Heaven upon their death in the physical world. **Color**: creamy white; **Crystal/Gemstone**: yellow calcite; **Astrological sign**: Capricorn

Chamuel (*Eyes of God*) helps us find something we've lost or are searching for (our keys, a job, our soulmate). He is also responsible for aiding in the manifestation of individual and universal peace. **Color**: pale green; **Crystal/Gemstone**: fluorite; **Astrological sign**: Taurus

Gabriel (*Strength of God*) guides our artistic and creative endeavors and can help with procrastination. She also specializes in pregnancy, birth, and adoption and supports sensitive children. **Color**: copper; **Crystal/Gemstone**: copper; **Astrological sign**: Cancer

Haniel (*Grace of God*) assists us in strengthening our spiritual gifts and intuition. She works with sacred feminine energy and specializes in women's issues. Call on her during a full moon for healing and release. **Color**: pale blue; **Crystal/Gemstone**: moonstone; **Astrological sign**: oversees all

Jeremiel (*Mercy of God*) is a mentor and teacher who helps us conduct a life review at any point along our path, as well as once we cross over. He also supports the development of our spiritual gifts. **Color**: dark purple; **Crystal/Gemstone**: amethyst; **Astrological sign**: Scorpio

Jophiel (*Beauty of God*) brings beauty to all aspects of life (your home, thoughts, Self). She can shift your mood from negative to positive and help with misunderstandings. **Color:** fuchsia or dark pink; **Crystal/Gemstone:** deep pink tourmaline or rubellite; **Astrological sign:** Libra

Metatron (*unknown*) "walked with God" during his mortal life as the prophet Enoch, one of only two archangels who ascended directly into the angelic realm. He is known for his use of sacred Geometry and his healing cube, the Merkabah, which clears away lower energies. He also assists us with time management and nurtures highly-sensitive and misunderstood children. **Color:** violet and green; **Crystal/Gemstone:** watermelon tourmaline; **Astrological sign:** Virgo

Michael (*He Who is Like God*) is arguably the most famous archangel. He helps us feel safe and protected, using his mighty sword to soothe our fears and provide us with clarity and self-confidence. **Color:** royal purple, royal blue, and gold; **Crystal/Gemstone:** sugulite; **Astrological sign:** oversees all

Raguel (*Friend of God*) heals misunderstandings and brings harmony, peace, and forgiveness to individuals or groups. His specialty is relationships, including the one we have with ourselves. **Color:** light blue; **Crystal/Gemstone:** aquamarine; **Astrological sign:** Sagittarius

Raphael (*God Heals*) is known as the angel of healing; call on him when sick or in pain. He also protects us while traveling and can serve as a matchmaker. **Color**: emerald green; **Crystal/Gemstone**: emerald or malachite; **Astrological sign**: oversees all

Raziel (*Secrets of God*) helps us gain esoteric wisdom, heal from past-life trauma, interpret dreams, and understand our life lessons. **Color**: rainbow colors; **Crystal/Gemstone**: clear quartz; **Astrological sign**: Leo

Sandalphon (*Brother Together*) lived on Earth as the prophet Elijah, ascending directly into the angelic realm, like Metatron. His height is said to span from Earth to Heaven, making him an excellent intercessor for prayers between the two. He is also the patron of musicians. **Color**: Turquoise; **Crystal/Gemstone**: turquoise; **Astrological sign**: Pisces

Uriel (*Light of God*) is said to have guided the prophet Enoch while he walked the Earth. He guides our ideas, insights, and intellectual pursuits. He works with Zadkiel to assist us with tests and schoolwork. **Color**: yellow; **Crystal/Gemstone**: amber; **Astrological sign**: Aquarius

Zadkiel (*Righteousness of God*) inspires forgiveness and compassion. He works with our mind to support memory, aid in our studies (along with Uriel), and heal past emotional pain. **Color**:

indigo blue; **Crystal/Gemstone**: lapis lazuli; **Astrological sign**: Gemini

Learning to communicate with the angels can enrich our lives in a multitude of ways, since each has an area of expertise. They can be used in all areas of life—education, healing, relationships, cultivating peace and beauty, protection, child-rearing...the list is endless. Even better, they are super easy to connect with. We can call on them by name, sense their energy, visualize their color, or even meditate with a particular crystal or gemstone. The neat thing is that the primary role of the archangels and our own guardian angels is to assist us during our earthly journey. That is why they exist. That being said, free will prevents them from intervening on our behalf unless we ask for their help. So, call upon them frequently—get to know them. They are available to everyone, and they're never too busy to help us.

Resources: Part Two

Books:

Psychical and Spiritual by Michael Perry

Our Mathematical Universe: My Quest for the Ultimate Nature of Reality by Max Tegmark

Glynis Has Your Number: Discover What Life Has in Store for You Through the Power of Numerology by Glynis McCants

Messages in the Numbers: The Universe is Talking to You by Alana Fairchild

Websites:

Churches' Fellowship for Psychical and Spiritual Studies (CFPSS):
http://www.churchesfellowship.co.uk/home/4594673287

What is Your Psychic Gift? (James Van Praagh):
https://www.vanpraagh.com/psychic-gift-test/

Radleigh Valentine: https://radleighvalentine.com/

Louise Hay: https://louisehay.com/

Gabby Bernstein: https://gabbybern:stein.com/

William Brown, psychic/medium/channel:
https://william-brown.com/

Lee Carroll, channel: https://www.menus.kryon.com/

Darryl Anka, channel: https://www.bashar.org/

Priscilla Keresey, psychic/medium:
http://www.apracticalpsychic.com/

Paul Selig, channel: https://paulselig.com/

Esther Hicks, channel: https://www.abraham-hicks.com/

Part Three: Healing

"Eventually you will come to understand that love heals everything, and love is all there is."
Gary Zukav

"True healing takes place within."
Unknown

As I mentioned in Chapter 1, my sincere spiritual exploration (outside of the Christian church) began with my gift of healing. After receiving my own *message from God* and creating a hands-on healing team for my church, I was led to Reiki, another form of hands-on healing. Although it was new to me, holistic healing (that which is outside of the established medical protocol) is not a new phenomenon. In fact, thousands of years ago, holistic healing was the ONLY medical treatment available. Before we delve into a description of a few common holistic healing practices, let's begin with some background about healing in general, as well as the history behind our modern forms of energy healing.

Origin of Wellness

The idea of 'wellness' is a fairly recent concept; however, its roots can be traced back thousands of years. Throughout history, a wide range of cultures accepted the notion that human beings were more than just skin and bones, blood, and muscle. They believed in the existence of a universal energy that permeated all living things, and that belief system served as the foundation for healing techniques that addressed a wide variety of medical issues. Our ancestors understood the relationship between man and earth, the physical and the non-physical, and they used that knowledge to sustain and heal themselves. Although Eastern medicine has long recognized those same ideas, in the West, it has only been relatively recently that the mainstream medical community has begun to accept and appreciate holistic medicine.

Perhaps the earliest evidence of holistic health practices can be seen in the herbal medicine traditions of the world. The use of plants as preventive and therapeutic medicine dates back to the origin of humankind. In fact, even carnivorous animals, such as the common housecats of today, are known to seek out and consume vegetation when ill. Over time, every culture in the world has developed an herbal knowledge base used for the prevention of illness, the healing of the body, or both. The first written evidence of medicinal herb use was found in ancient Mesopotamia (present day Iraq) and dates back 5,000 years to the ancient Sumerians. Archeologists uncovered clay tablets on which prescriptions for healing herbs, such as caraway and thyme, had been written.

The tenets of our current concept of wellness can be traced back to the early civilizations of Greece, Rome, and Asia. One of the earliest examples of holistic medicine is Ayurveda, the ancient medical tradition of India that dates back to 3000-1500 BC and which gave birth to our modern practices of yoga and meditation. Ayurveda began as an oral tradition that was later recorded into four sacred, spiritual, and philosophical Hindu texts called the Vedas. This system tailors its practice to the unique needs of each individual, while remaining focused on the overall balance and harmony of body, mind, and spirit.

Traditional Chinese Medicine (TCM), with its roots in Taoism and Buddhism, originated between 3000-2000 BC. TCM is a complex system of diagnostic and treatment practices that regards the body as an interconnected web of processes and systems, not unlike a small universe. Similar to Ayurveda, TCM focused on the cultivation and maintenance of a balance between the physical and spiritual aspects of the Self. TCM practitioners recognize the body's vital energy, called the *chi* or *qi*, a universal, life force energy that animates all living things. Many of our current practices today, such as Acupuncture and Tai Chi, evolved from TCM.

The ancient Greek physician Hippocrates, who lived in the fourth century BC, believed in the healing power of nature, as well as the natural instinct of our own body to heal itself. With a strong focus on prevention, his recommendations included a healthy diet and lifestyle, as well as the inclusion of environmental considerations in the treatment process. Early Roman medicine, around 50 BC, also adopted this concept of prevention over intervention. The Romans were able to make the connection between the causes of disease and methods of prevention. This revelation led to the development of the first public health system, comprised of aqueducts, sewers, and public baths, which prevented the spread of disease through personal and environmental cleanliness.

In spite of Hippocrates' focus on prevention, many of his colleagues continued to concentrate on the treatment of symptoms. For centuries, the debate raged on between the two approaches - prevention versus intervention. In the mid to late 1800s however, the discovery of disease-causing germs signaled a turning point in the way Western medicine viewed prevention. Instead of relying solely on symptom mitigation, doctors were now able to find and treat the source of the symptom. In spite of this new information, physicians were still not very attentive to the role of environment, lifestyle, or emotions on one's health. In fact, the discovery of revolutionary medicines like penicillin actually discouraged patients from participating in their own health care. They were now able to sit back and let their doctor *cure* them with these miraculous new drugs.

In the early 1900s, John Harvey Kellogg, director of a Sanatorium in Michigan suggested that patients who ate well, exercised, breathed in fresh air, and engaged in hydrotherapy (the use of heat, cold, steam, or ice to relieve pain) were more likely to remain in good health. Around this same time, the practice of naturopathy—encouraging the body to heal itself through things like diet, lifestyle, herbs, and massage—spread to the U.S. from Europe. Theories, such as detoxification and anthroposophical medicine (balancing the mind/body/spirit), were suggested as holistic health options, as well. Despite this progress, in 1910, the Carnegie Foundation published the Flexner report, a document intended to overhaul America's medical schools, aligning them with Germany's hyper-rational medical system. This single publication created an overemphasis on scientific protocols and questioned the validity of holistic practices, thus setting the stage for our modern-day, disease-oriented, drug-reliant medical perspective.

Wellness Today

Slowly but surely, the interest in holistic health returned, and by the 1970s, the foundation had been laid for our modern concept of wellness. The first National Conference on Holistic Health was held in California in 1975, and the formation of the American Holistic Health Association (AHHA) and the Holistic Medical Association (HMA) occurred soon after. From the 1980s through the 2000s, momentum was building in the medical, corporate, and academic arenas. Employers began to provide wellness programs, the fitness and spa industry took off, and celebrity gurus thrust the concept of health and wellness onto the national stage. The US National Center for Complementary and Alternative Medicine (NCCAM) was established in 1991, falling under the National Institutes of Health, and by the early twenty-first century, wellness had reached its tipping point.

Today, the wellness movement has permeated every area of our lives, from travel to food and beverage and entertainment. More than half of all employers in the world utilize some type of health promotion strategy, with a third of them being full-blown wellness programs. Research by the Global Wellness Institute (GWI), an organization founded in 2014, revealed that the global wellness industry, comprising ten divisions, including Complementary & Alternative Medicine, Beauty & Anti-Aging, Nutrition & Weight Loss, Fitness & Mind-Body and others, is now a $34 trillion market.

Holistic Medicine

To develop a thorough understanding of holistic medicine, we need to define the various approaches to healthcare.

Conventional Medicine: The exclusive use of traditional Western medical practices.

Alternative Medicine: The exclusive use of healing treatments and therapies not practiced in conventional, Western medicine.

Complementary Approach: The use of alternative therapies in concert with conventional medicine.

Holistic or Integrative Approach: The patient-centered use of healing techniques and practices derived from multiple disciplines (traditional and/or non-traditional).

In general, most current Western holistic or integrative practitioners operate from a similar philosophy: a belief in the healing power of unconditional love, a desire to nurture a symbiotic, cooperative relationship with their patients, and an interdisciplinary approach to healing, using both traditional and complementary techniques. They believe that healing is most effective when the whole person is considered, as opposed to the traditional focus on illness, symptoms, and body parts in isolation. Holistic health, therefore, is a state of balance and well-being, not just an absence of disease. There is an appreciation for and an understanding of the relationship between the body, mind, spirit, and environment.

Complementary, alternative, and/or non-traditional techniques run the gamut from chiropractic and massage to yoga, acupuncture, and holistic nutrition. The National Center for Complementary and Integrative Health (NCCIH)—a branch of the National Institutes of Health (NIH) that falls under the US Department of Health and Human Services—organized these practices into five categories:

Alternative Medical Systems are healing systems developed outside of the traditional western medical approach. Examples are Chinese Medicine and Ayurveda.

Mind-Body Interventions include behavioral, psychological, social, and spiritual approaches. Examples are cancer support groups and relaxation classes.

Natural Products include a wide variety of dietary supplements, herbs, vitamins, minerals, and probiotics. Examples are herbal medicines and aromatherapy.

Manipulative and Body-Based Methods use manipulation, touch, or movement of the physical body. Examples include massage therapy and chiropractic.

Energy Medicine involves some form of energy to heal, including electromagnetic, ultrasonic, thermal, or subtle energy. Examples include Healing Touch and Reiki.

The good news is that energy medicine and other holistic and alternative therapies are officially recognized by the US healthcare system. For the purposes of this book, we will focus on category five, energy medicine. Specifically, those practices that draw upon the universal life-force energy (introduced in Chapter 4), with the intention of healing the body, mind, and spirit.

What is Energy Medicine?

Energy medicine, according to The International Society for the Study of Subtle Energy and Energy Medicine (ISSSEEM), assumes three things: 1) Energetic imbalances can occur that result from an interaction between the mind *and* the body; 2) we can diagnose these energetic imbalances; and 3) once diagnosed, we can subsequently treat them. Energy medicine works within the *biofield*, described by the NIH as a combination of (measurable) electromagnetic energy and (unmeasurable) subtle energy. This field is also referred to as the Human Energy Field or *aura*.

Although Western science has not yet been able to formally describe or measure subtle energy, Eastern traditions have long recognized and written about its importance. As mentioned earlier, this subtle energy is known as *qi* or *chi* (*ki* in Japanese), the life-force energy that animates all living things. In Ayurveda, this energy is called *prana*. Our energetic body is comprised of seven main energy centers, or *chakras*, aligned along the spine, from its base up to the crown of the head. These spinning wheels of energy are where matter meets consciousness (chakras are covered in more detail in Chapter 16). *Nadis* (referred to as *meridians* in Chinese medicine), which are small channels or tubes, connect to the chakras and carry *prana* throughout the energetic body. The entire process is a bit more complex; however, this short description provides enough of a foundation to understand the energetic healing practices in this section.

A Brief History of Energy Medicine

After the Flexner report put the kibosh on new research into alternative health practices, it took several decades to rebuild momentum. A few dedicated pioneers, however, did manage to conduct some encouraging studies. Nicola Tesla, in a paper presented in 1898, asserted that the high frequency currents produced by his Tesla coils could be used for healing. In 1916, Dr. Albert Abrams wrote about the "vibratory rate" of diseases and maintained that these transmissions could be measured and treated. From 1932-1956, Dr. Harold Burr at Yale University investigated the energy fields of living organisms which he called "L" fields. Burr believed that diseases could be detected—and healed—in this energy field prior to their manifestation in the physical body. With each of these new discoveries, researchers steadily began to lay the groundwork for the energy medicine of today.

Although the term *energy medicine* didn't appear on the scene until the late 1980s, the concepts were gaining momentum in the West by the 1940s. German physician, Dr. Reinhold Voll, identified specific areas on the skin—now known as acupuncture points—that displayed significantly decreased electrical resistance compared to surrounding areas. One of Voll's colleagues, Dr. Franz Morrell, theorized that healthy bodies produced specific electromagnetic signals, perceived as smooth waves of information. Disease, he said, caused disruptions in these waves. Morrell's subsequent research involved the manipulation of these irregular wave forms in order to restore health.

In 1963, Gerhard Baule and Richard McFee at Syracuse University were able to detect the bio-magnetic field emanating from the human heart, using two coils, two million turns of wire and a sensitive amplifier. This was significant discovery! Until that time, although it was known that tissues and cells generate an electrical field along with a corresponding magnetic field, the magnetic field had evaded detection. It had simply been too small to measure. By 1972, David Cohen at the Massachusetts Institute of Technology was able to use a SQUID magnetometer to measure the magnetic fields around not only the heart but the head, as well. The 1970s also brought an upsurge in attention surrounding biofeedback and subtle body energy systems, as well as TCM practices, such as acupuncture. Since that time, the number of American researchers investigating the topics of subtle energy and energy medicine has increased dramatically.

Energy Medicine Today

Dr. C. Norman Shealy, chair emeritus of the energy medicine program at Greenwich University in Australia, is credited with bringing energy medicine into the mainstream during the 1980s through his research on and subsequent training of *medical intuitives*. In fact, Dr. Shealy and bestselling author, Carolyn Myss, Ph.D. (one of his students) actually coined the term *medical intuitive*. A medical intuitive is a person, typically without medical training, who is able to sense or *intuit* an individual's health condition by detecting disturbances in the energy field. The International Society for the Study of Subtle Energy and Energy Medicine, founded in 1989, played a huge role in advancing the field of energy medicine through the publication of their quarterly magazine, *Bridges,* and the peer-reviewed, scholarly journal,

Subtle Energies and Energy Medicine. (Although the publications were discontinued in 1991, the archives are still available online.)

In the 1990s, mainstream doctors Christiane Northrop, M.D. (*Women's Bodies, Women's Wisdom*), Mona Lisa Schultz, M.D. (*Awakening Intuition*), and Judith Orloff, M.D. (*Second Sight*), published works that included the topics of energy anatomy, intuitive healing, and the use of clairvoyance in psychiatry, respectively. More recently, the pioneering work of biologist Bruce Lipton, Ph.D. helped to reinforce the bridge between science and spirituality. His 2005 book, *The Biology of Belief: Unleashing the Power of Consciousness, Matter and Miracles,* laid the foundation for a consciousness-based understanding of biology and thrust the concept of *epigenetics* into the mainstream. Epigenetics examines the factors that cause our genes to switch on and off, which subsequently determines how our cells read those genes. Lipton's research demonstrates that our health is not at the mercy of heredity. On the contrary, he asserts, our bodies are positively influenced by our thoughts (and thoughts are energy, remember?).

Thanks to other well-known Western medical doctors, such as Deepak Chopra, Dean Ornish, Brian Weiss, Andrew Weil, and Mehmet Oz, alternative healing practices, including energy medicine, have garnered even more attention. Oprah Winfrey elevated these practitioners, and many others, to celebrity status by promoting their platforms on her television show. According to US News and World Report almost half of all American adults today believe in the value of complementary and alternative medicine, or CAM.

As a testament to the increased interest in CAM, medical school membership in The Consortium of Academic Health Centers for Integrative Medicine, which was founded in 2000, jumped from eight to forty-six in ten years. A growing number of medical students are learning about herbal remedies and meditation in addition to Anatomy and Physiology. Indeed, eighty-seven medical schools now offer some type of CAM curricula. Even the Veterans Administration (VA) has gotten on board in its attempt to address the increasing numbers of veterans returning from overseas conflicts with severe medical and psychological disorders. In Charleston, South Carolina, for example, the VA picks up the tab for service-disabled veterans to receive acupuncture treatments and suggests that they attend a pain management seminar—four hours of information on alternative therapies for the treatment of chronic pain.

Energy medicine has come a long way, particularly over the past twenty years. Because it is such a broad topic—it can include electromagnetic, ultrasonic, thermal, or subtle energy—this section will include only those practices that rely on subtle or universal life force energy. In the following chapters, we will discuss some of the most commonly practiced energy healing modalities.

Disclaimer: *Although I have a Dr. in front of my name, I am not a medical doctor, and it is not my intent to provide medical advice. All of the practices listed in this section are meant to be supplemental to, and used in cooperation with, traditional medical and/or psychological treatments, as part of a comprehensive, holistic health plan. Please consult with a medical doctor prior to practicing any of these modalities.*

Chapter 12 - Acupuncture and Acupressure

Acupuncture, and its cousin, Acupressure, are two holistic modalities widely practiced and accepted within traditional Western medicine. That is probably why, although I didn't understand what lots of tiny needles had to do with healing, I wasn't fearful of acupuncture…at least not from a religious perspective. Petrified of shots, however, I wasn't about to pay someone to stick a bunch of needles into my body, tiny or not. Who would do that? Truth be told, I ultimately did experience a traditional acupuncture treatment about a year ago. Much to my surprise, it wasn't at all uncomfortable. I also tried Electro-acupuncture (described below), at the request of my "mainstream" orthopedist, for a backache I was dealing with. While not painful, the stimulation was an odd feeling. And, although both sessions seemed to alleviate my symptoms, at least temporarily, my busy schedule prevented me from maintaining a consistent course of treatment.

What is Acupuncture?

Acupuncture, a traditional Chinese medicine (TCM) technique, has been practiced for thousands of years. Early Chinese writings as far back as 100 BC, describe a system of diagnosis and treatment using needles, although the modality is most likely older than this written record. The process changed a great deal over time, and by the eighteenth century, the practice of acupuncture looked much different than it did in those early writings. And, by the early twentieth century, aspiring Chinese doctors were no longer studying acupuncture. However, in the 1950s and 1960s, due to an increasing population and a decreasing supply of doctors in China, the Communist leadership began promoting acupuncture again, as a way to provide healthcare to the masses.

Like Qigong and Tai Chi, the practice of acupuncture is based on the premise that illness is rooted in a blockage within our body's energy system. Thus, the goal of the acupuncturist is to remove or release those energy blocks, allowing the energy to flow freely again. However, the acupuncture that is practiced currently, particularly in the West, is no longer based on those early principles. Today, acupuncture has become a popular, if misunderstood, practice for pain relief and symptom reduction that doesn't rely on medication.

What is Acupressure?

Acupressure is similar to acupuncture in purpose and process. Rather than needles, however, acupressure uses manual pressure from the practitioner's hands, typically a thumb, knuckle, or finger, to stimulate the points along the body. Acupressure treatments can be provided by a practitioner or self-administered. Each point on the body is stimulated for one to two minutes at a time, with the process being repeated three to five times. To provide more consistent treatment, clients are often sent home with an acupressure wristband, an adjustable band that has a small bead sewn into it that is designed to put constant pressure on the P-6 acupressure point at the wrist. Very often, this is used in cases of nausea and vomiting caused by motion sickness, morning sickness, cancer treatments, or surgery anesthesia. Acupressure patches have also been created that work in a similar fashion to the band, providing ongoing stimulation to the acupressure point.

Reflexology is a type of acupressure that focuses on the hands and feet, which have their own acupressure points, called *reflexes*. Each reflex point is energetically connected to a particular body part or organ system. For example, the tips of the toes reflect the head, and the ball of the foot corresponds to the heart and chest. The roots of reflexology, similar to acupuncture and acupressure, can be traced back to ancient China. However, the concept of *zone therapy* is much newer, being introduced in 1915 by William H. Fitzgerald and subsequently expanded upon by an American physiotherapist, Eunice Ingram, in the 1930s. It was this early practice of zone therapy that paved the way for we now know as Reflexology.

How they Work

Acupuncture works through the placement of tiny needles at key places on the body, called acupuncture points. There are over 1,000 of these points, and they lie along invisible energy channels, called meridians. Each meridian is responsible for a different organ system of the body. By stimulating specific acupuncture points along the appropriate meridian, blockages within the energy path can be removed so that the energy is able to flow freely again. Researchers, looking for a scientific explanation, believe that the process is related to the release of endorphins and/or the release of chemicals that regulate blood flow when these points are stimulated. With regard to acupressure, the assumption is that the pressure applied to the acupressure points interrupts the pain signal to the nervous system.

Not only can acupuncture be done with needles, now there are techniques called Laser acupuncture and Electro-acupuncture, whereby the acupuncture needles are stimulated with lasers or with an electrical device that provides a weak electric current. For those who suffer from insomnia or who are seeking to lose weight or stop smoking, a practitioner might suggest auriculo-acupuncture, which involves needles placed only in the ear.

Prior to a treatment, your acupuncturist will gather some background information: symptoms, expectations, diet, stress level, and so on. The practitioner will also note your pulse, tongue color and coating, and other aspects of your appearance; in Chinese medicine, these indicators can reflect the condition or health of your organs and systems. Treatments take place sitting or lying down on a massage table. The practitioner will typically use six to fifteen needles per treatment, and they are left in for ten to twenty minutes, sometimes longer. The needles may be twisted to aid in the stimulation of the acupuncture points. After a session, it is important to drink water to assist with the energy flow, and you may be encouraged to rest, if possible.

How they Can Help

Both acupuncture and acupressure have been shown to positively impact a variety of issues, such as headaches/migraines, nausea, and stress. In 2016 alone, two separate studies demonstrated a decrease in the frequency of migraine episodes and tension headaches. In another study, completed in 2017, patients reported that acupuncture decreased their back pain, and a fourth study indicated a reduction in knee pain when consistent acupuncture treatments were provided. Acupuncture, specifically, is often used to promote fertility and to treat addictions, like smoking. Other health conditions that acupuncture can be used to address include anxiety, depression, and insomnia, arthritis, weight loss, tinnitus, and sinus congestion. In addition, acupressure has been correlated with a reduction in muscle tension and pain, menstrual cramps, and cancer-related fatigue. What many studies fail to report is the overarching benefit that is gained from using a holistic approach to pain management versus medication that can have side-effects. Holistic practices, like acupuncture and acupressure can assist in addressing the root cause of the issue, rather than simply treating a symptom.

Chapter 13 - Craniosacral Therapy

Craniosacral therapy (CST) is a non-invasive, alternative modality often practiced by osteopaths, chiropractors, and massage therapists. As such, it has a plethora of followers, but a fair share of critics, as well. As touched on earlier, with regard to most of the healing techniques described in this section, concrete scientific data is hard to come by; therefore, proponents often base their opinions on the positive personal experiences they've had. At present, researchers simply haven't developed instruments with a level of sensitivity that can detect and measure the subtle workings of our body's energy field. Although I can't personally speak to its long-term effectiveness, I can say that the one CST session I received was soothing and comforting. I left feeling noticeably lighter.

What is CST?

CST traces its roots back to the work of an osteopathic physician named William Garner Sutherland during the early 1900s. It is important to note (as it lends credibility to the practice of CST) that a Doctor of Osteopathic Medicine (DO) is a licensed medical practitioner, having received the same rigorous training as an MD. Both MDs and DOs possess the legal authority to diagnose and treat health conditions, prescribe medication, and perform surgery. The difference between the two is that the osteopath focuses on the *whole person*, with a particular emphasis on the relationship between the musculoskeletal system and the disease or symptom. Not only do osteopaths complete the same curriculum as MDs, schools of osteopathic medicine provide an additional 300 to 500 hours of specialized training in the musculoskeletal system.

As a senior at the American School of Osteopathy, Dr. Sutherland was particularly intrigued by the bones of the cranium. Although he was taught that these bones fuse in adulthood, their very structure implied the opposite—that they were designed for movement. This concept triggered a lifelong exploration into the potential for motion within the skull and whether this motion had any impact on human physiology. Over the course of many years, Sutherland endeavored to describe his experiences in biomechanical language and create processes to release what he considered to be resistance in the cranial structures. His work took a dramatic turn in 1945, however, when he discovered what he called the Breath of Life, an intelligent energetic force that is housed within every human being. Essentially, Sutherland had discovered, and personally experienced, what we now know as *qi*, *chi*, or *prana*.

This new revelation changed the way Sutherland viewed *treatment*. No longer did he rely on the application of techniques that he considered to be *force from the outside*. Instead, he understood that, through intention, the practitioner could assist the client's own energy field to create the conditions for healing.

The practitioners that have followed in Dr. Sutherland's footsteps eventually branched out into two distinct schools of thought, the biomechanical and biodynamic approach. And, although each approach produces changes within the body and mind, they are very different.

In the 1970s, Dr. John Upledger designed a specific *biomechanical* framework for the practice of CST that resulted in the establishment of a defined CST profession that could operate outside of the osteopathic community. His work, through the Upledger Institute, is still taught all over the world. His biomechanical approach seeks to correct imbalances in the client's system by way of gentle hand pressure. It focuses on three areas of movement: within the bones of the head; between the bones of the pelvis, at the sacrum; and the flow of fluid around the brain and spinal cord.

Around the same time, Franklyn Sills became intrigued by the work of Randolph Stone, DO, who himself had been a huge devotee of Dr. Sutherland. Stone, at that time, was researching what he referred to as *primary energy*. Seeking to learn more, Sills eventually moved to England, undertook osteopathic training, and co-founded the Karuna Institute in 1982. By 1986, Sills, along with his colleague Claire Dolby, DO, began teaching a course that included the biomechanical language of CST, as well as a technique that accessed the client's Breath of Life. The

Karuna classes, therefore, approached CST from not only the biomechanical aspect but from a *biodynamic* one.

Students soon realized, however, that in practice, their treatments were not really focused on the mechanics of the process. Rather, the primary catalyst for healing was the regenerative power of the life force energy. In other words, healing came from the client (from the inside), not the practitioner (from the outside). In order for the training to accurately reflect what was being practiced, Sills eliminated the biomechanical component, creating what is now known as Biodynamic Craniosacral Therapy (BCST). Sills' students began teaching in the United States in 1995, and in 1998, in order to support the growing number of practitioners, the Biodynamic Craniosacral Therapy Association of North America was created.

How it Works

As with any type of healthcare, a CST session begins with a consultation. The practitioner should request a health history, ask about present concerns, explain the therapeutic process, and discuss expectations. Sessions most often take place while lying on a massage table, fully clothed, and the CST practitioner may ask questions throughout the session to ensure that the process is flowing smoothly and comfortably. During a CST treatment, the practitioner taps into the subtle rhythms of the client's system by gently holding various parts of the body, such as the feet, head, and sacrum. The therapist listens to the body's expressions, which help pinpoint areas of imbalance. During a CST session, clients may experience mild physical sensations when stagnant energy is released. Many people report feeling extremely relaxed and may experience a sense of warmth, softening, or floating. Depending upon the client's concerns, a session might last anywhere from thirty to ninety minutes. After the treatment, the client and practitioner should discuss the experience and determine the need for a follow up. While a single session can have a profound effect, as is the case with most holistic modalities, repeated visits often provide longer-lasting results.

How it Can Help

Due to the gentle, non-invasive nature of CST, virtually anyone can benefit from a treatment. A session can leave a client feeling lighter, deeply relaxed, and centered. Because CST utilizes the body's energetic field, it can be helpful for not only the physical manifestation of a disorder but also any related emotional trauma. For example, injuries, accidents, or surgeries not only affect us physically; they can leave an energetic residue as a result of anesthesia or stress that can be addressed within a CST session. CST is safe for children and the elderly, as well as pregnant women. In fact, this modality can be particularly beneficial during pregnancy, as it can calm the nervous system of both mother and child and lead to a strengthening of their emotional bond.

A CST session can be a wonderful preventative therapy because it facilitates the restoration of energetic imbalances within the body that, if left untreated, could manifest as physical illness. The Upledger Institute asserts that CST is a suitable option for the treatment of immune disorders, such as chronic fatigue and fibromyalgia (a 2010 study upheld this claim, demonstrating a reduction of pain in fibromyalgia patients); head and spinal issues, such as concussion, migraines, spinal cord injury, and scoliosis; childhood complications, such as colic, autism, and learning disabilities; as well as issues of the elderly, such as dementia and Alzheimer's. Other studies found CST helpful in the reduction of asthma symptoms, as well as the complications of multiple sclerosis. CST has also been used to successfully address emotional issues like PTSD, anxiety, depression, and trauma. According to the University of Minnesota, CST can inspire change in a client's overall perspective of health and wellbeing. In short, CST practitioners recognize that the human body is beautifully capable of repatterning toward health; a CST session might just provide the perfect opportunity for that process to begin.

Chapter 14 - Reiki

As you learned in Chapter 1, Reiki training was my first introduction to a *formal* holistic healing protocol. As a Christian, I was afraid of it. In fact, it took me *four years* of exploration—asking questions, reading about it, having a Reiki treatment—to conclude that I was being drawn to practice Reiki. When I finally decided to attend Reiki level I training I was excited but still a bit nervous. It was a very deliberate step not only outside of my comfort zone but one that was in direct conflict with the Christian belief system I had been raised with. I realize that even Christians have vastly different views on all sorts of topics; we discussed that in Chapter 2. Perhaps for some of you, energy healing of this type is not considered taboo, but for me, it most definitely was.

So there I was, sitting in my Reiki Master's living room, completely out of my element but feeling strangely calm. There were three other students, all of whom were much more relaxed and familiar with alternative spiritual practices. I wondered what my mother would have said had she still been alive. No doubt, she would have been gravely concerned for my soul. By then, however, I had already ditched the idea that our souls only live once and upon death, end up in Heaven or Hell. In reality, I knew that my mom was with me in Spirit, watching over me, probably super excited that I was pursuing my gift of healing.

Deep down, I felt that she would support me in this work, more than she ever could have while she was alive.

As I looked around the room, I gazed upon a number of unfamiliar objects—an elephant (Ganesh) and a framed picture of Dr. Usui, founder of Reiki, along with a deck of Tarot cards and a set of Runes (although, at the time, I didn't know what they were) lying on the table. Luckily, I also saw a picture of Jesus, sitting alongside Dr. Usui, although I silently wondered how Jesus would feel about that. I was curious as to how my Reiki Master would intertwine the Jesus of my Christian faith with the practice of Reiki. The group chatted amiably about various types of essential oils and oracle card decks, as I sat in a state of wide-eyed bewilderment. My new friends found my naivety quite amusing. As we worked together over the next two days, my inexperience and apprehension would be the subject of loads of good-natured ribbing. Nevertheless, my experiences during the Reiki I and subsequent Reiki classes were profound and changed the trajectory of my life.

Although it was developed by a Buddhist, Reiki is not affiliated with any religion. Healing, through the laying on of hands, however, is a deeply embedded Christian tradition. In fact, Jesus was well known for healing the sick, very often through the power of touch. For example, Jesus healed Peter's feverish mother-in-law by touching her (Matthew 8:14-15) and with his hands, healed a man of leprosy (Mark 1:40-42). Jesus healed two blind men by touching their eyes (Matthew 20:29-34), as well as a deaf man with a speech impediment, after touching the man's ears and tongue (Mark 7:32-35). In yet another example, Jesus resuscitated a dead girl through the power of touch (Luke 8:49-55). After laying His hands on a woman who had been crippled for 18 years, Jesus cured her affliction, and she stood erect again (Luke 13:11-13). Paul was also said to have brought about a healing after laying his hands on a man afflicted with fever and dysentery (Acts 28:8).

In addition to Jesus's direct examples of healing touch, the Bible describes healing as being a Gift of the Spirit. In 1 Corinthians 12:4-12, Paul tells of these gifts, which include speaking in tongues and having the power to heal. Paul also describes the people of the church as having various roles, such as prophets, teachers, and healers (1 Corinthians 12:28-31). Because healing is considered to be a spiritual gift, granted by God, Biblical scholars assert that the supernatural healing of the sick should remain a core ministry of the Church. Many Christian denominations use the laying on of hands not only for healing but to invoke the Holy Spirit. Acts 8:17 confirms this: "Then they laid hands on them, and they received the Holy Spirit." This practice is common during religious ceremonies, including baptisms, confirmations, and ordinations and in the commission of missionaries prior to their field work.

Many Christian Reiki practitioners trust that they have been called by God, through the Holy Spirit, to practice the gift of healing. They feel confident that they are following Jesus's example and are encouraged by his words: "Most assuredly, I say to you, he who believes in Me, the works that I do he will do also; and greater works than these he will do, because I go to My Father" (John 14:12). These practitioners believe in the power of touch and have been drawn to Reiki as their healing modality. The Reiki energy, in their view, emanates from the same Source as the energy being called upon and utilized during Christian healings and ceremonies.

What is Reiki?

Reiki is a spiritual healing technique that was developed in 1922 by Dr. Mikao Usui, a Japanese Buddhist. The word Reiki is formed from a combination of the Japanese words *Rei*, which means Universal Life, and *Ki*, which means Energy. Reiki, therefore, is the energetic, universal life force that animates all living things. This energy is transferred from practitioner to client through the hands, either placed on the client's body or positioned slightly above the body. Although Reiki is spiritual in nature, it is not affiliated with any religious practice or dogma, and it is said to work regardless of the client's belief in it. Reiki practitioner training is comprised of three levels, Reiki I, II, and III. Reiki III training is further divided into two parts, Master/Practitioner and Master/Teacher. During each training level, the Reiki Master provides students with an *attunement*—an unlocking of the ability to channel the Reiki energy.

Hawayo Takata is credited with bringing Usui Reiki to the United States. Mrs. Takata, whose parents were Japanese immigrants, was born and raised on the island of Kauai, Hawaii. As an adult, she traveled back to Japan to attend her sister's funeral and seek treatment for a number of health ailments. Rather than undergo surgery, as suggested by her physicians, Mrs. Takata sought assistance from Dr. Chujiro Hayashi, one of Usui's original 16 initiated Reiki teachers. After being treated at Hyashi's clinic for 4 months, Mrs. Takata was completely healed. Anxious to learn this healing technique herself, she trained with Dr Hyashi for over a year, eventually returning to Hawaii in 1937. Hyashi and his daughter followed shortly after. Together, the three enabled this healing practice to flourish in the US. Although Usui Reiki is considered to be the most widely practiced technique, well over 150 styles of Reiki have since been developed, according to William Lee Rand, founder of the International Center for Reiki Training (ICRT).

How it Works

Like the other practices in this section, the Reiki practitioner works to restore proper energy flow and balance in the client's body. It is a noninvasive practice, with no contraindications. A Reiki treatment is similar to a massage in that the client typically lies on a massage table for a session lasting approximately sixty to ninety minutes. Unlike a massage, however, the client remains fully clothed, aside from removing the shoes.

The Reiki practitioner, following Usui's protocol, will place his/her hands in specific locations on the body during the session—head, shoulders/neck, abdomen, feet, and the back, depending on the client's needs—but may also work on other body parts at the client's request, such as a sore knee. The hand placements are intended to correspond to each of the seven chakras (energy centers in the body), which in turn, are associated with specific organs and body systems. At the request of the client or based on the preference of the practitioner, a hands-off approach may be used, whereby the practitioner will hold his/her hands slightly above the body, working in the aura (the energy field surrounding the body).

Although there is an official protocol for Usui Reiki treatments, many practitioners develop their own techniques, based on an intuitive sense of the client's needs and/or their own experience regarding the way the energy works through them. Reiki can also be practiced on oneself, using the hand-placement protocol for self-treatment. This requires the Reiki level I attunement, however.

Prior to a Reiki treatment, the practitioner should conduct a thorough initial consultation with the client to discuss the process, the client's background, physical/emotional concerns, level of comfort, and other pertinent topics. The practitioner may also inquire as to the client's treatment goals. During the Reiki treatment, the client may experience warmth, tingling, floating, or nothing at all, other than a deep feeling of relaxation. Each session and client experience is unique. At the end of the treatment, the practitioner will speak with the client to compare notes, sharing any information or impressions received during the session. S/he may discuss the need for a follow up treatment; as with most holistic interventions, multiple treatments generally result in better outcomes. It is also suggested that the recipient stay hydrated, as the energy will continue to work to release tension and stress and eliminate it from the body.

How it Can Help

The purpose of a Reiki session is to reduce stress, tension, and anxiety in order to induce the body's natural healing ability. Healing may take place on the physical, emotional, mental, or spiritual level. The energy is said to be intuitive, in that it knows where the healing needs to take place. Although a single Reiki session can result in an immediate, spontaneous healing, Reiki more commonly works through a gentle process over time, helping to harmonize the energy of the body, mind, and spirit. In this way, the Reiki energy addresses any underlying imbalance that may result in the manifestation of a symptom, rather than attempting to treat the symptom itself. Reiki works in harmony with all other kinds of treatment. One can continue to receive regular medical or psychological treatment while receiving Reiki, often with improved results. In fact, Reiki has been known to shorten healing time, reduce or eliminate pain, reduce stress, and create optimism. Often, patients who receive Reiki leave the hospital earlier than those who don't and have fewer complications.

Reiki is quickly becoming a widely recognized holistic treatment modality and is currently being practiced in many prestigious hospitals, including Columbia University Medical Center, Duke University, Yale New Haven Children's Hospital, New York Presbyterian Hospital, Memorial Sloan-Kettering Cancer Center, and the Dana Farber Cancer Institute. Reiki has also gotten the attention of the Department of Defense and the Veterans Administration (VA) as a complementary treatment for veterans suffering from PTSD and other disorders. Most notably, it is utilized in the Ft. Bliss Warrior Resilience Program and the Charleston, South Carolina, VA hospital and surrounding clinics. Seattle, Washington, is home to the Reiki Training Program, a program that is fully funded by the Washington State VA that trains veterans to become Reiki practitioners themselves.

Chapter 15 - Tapping Therapy

How would you like to have an acupuncture treatment that was not only free, but free of needles, as well? In essence, that is what you get with tapping! Tapping is a painless, self-administered holistic modality that costs nothing, is quick and easy, and can be done anywhere at any time. How can it get better than that?

What is Tapping Therapy?

Tapping Therapy (called *tapping* for short) is a method that can be used to address physical and emotional pain in the body. It was discovered by accident in 1980 by Roger Callahan, a psychologist who had been treating a client named Mary, suffering from a severe phobia of water. Even after a year of treatment, Mary was not making a great deal of progress. During one session, Mary sat in close proximity of a pool, attempting to control her anxiety through traditional psychotherapeutic techniques; however, she was still feeling tension—unresolved anxiety—in her gut. Dr. Callahan had studied Chinese medicine and remembered that the cheekbone was an acupuncture point for the stomach. In a flash of inspiration, he asked Mary to tap her cheekbone, thinking it might relieve her stomach pain. Not only did the pain disappear, Mary's water phobia vanished as well!

Buoyed by this miraculous turn of events, Dr. Callahan worked to explore and refine his newfound technique, which he called Thought Field Therapy (TFT). TFT required that practitioners tap on a specific sequence of meridian points depending upon on the particular issue the client was experiencing. Naturally, this was time consuming because the practitioner had to first diagnose the problem and then prescribe the appropriate tapping sequence. As time went on, the TFT method was gradually improved upon, most significantly by one of Callahan's students, Gary Craig. During the 1990s, Craig noticed that even in cases where the client's issue was misdiagnosed or the tapping sequence was not followed exactly, the client still improved. Craig ultimately realized that success was not related to the order in which the client tapped the meridian points. Based on this new revelation, Craig developed his own version of Callahan's process, calling it the Emotional Freedom Technique (EFT). Unlike TFT, EFT offers only one basic tapping sequence, regardless of the client's situation.

How it Works

Pain, whether emotional or physical, can get stored in the energetic system of the body. What's more, our emotionality and physicality are intricately linked by way of a feedback loop—physical symptoms of disease cause emotional distress, while unresolved emotional problems can actually cause physical symptoms. Tapping enables the body to release stored pain by disrupting the negative flow of energy and rewiring the energetic corridors. The stimulation of specific points on the body interrupts the old neural pathways that carry pain and trauma and creates new pathways that support healing. We can literally *tap into* our body's own healing power.

As we learned in Chapter 12, acupuncture works by stimulating certain points along invisible energy channels called meridians, allowing the energy to move freely again. Tapping takes that idea and modifies it a bit. Instead of using needles, you use your own fingertips to stimulate nine specific acupressure points. Taps are typically performed five to seven times on each location, with the dominant hand, using either two fingers, on small locations like the eyebrow, or four fingers, on larger areas like the top of the head. One round of tapping is complete when all nine of the points have been tapped on. EFT is divided into five steps:

Step One: *Determine the issue.* Identify the underlying fear, emotion, pain, or belief that needs to be released; this will serve as the focal point while you are tapping. (It is best to concentrate on only one issue at a time.) Rate the intensity of the fear/pain/belief on a scale from 1 (least intense) to 10 (most intense). This is your baseline and will help you monitor your progress after completing an EFT sequence.

Step Two: *Establish a setup phrase.* Prior to tapping, you will want to create a statement that encompasses both the issue you identified and an affirmation. A common statement is:

"Even though I have this [fear/pain/belief], I deeply and completely accept myself."

The statement must focus on your own state of being. For example, rather than saying, *"Even though my spouse is sick . . ."* you might phrase it this way, *"Even though I'm anxious about my spouse's illness . . ."* In other words, focus on how the issue makes *you* feel.

Step Three: *Begin the tapping sequence.* First, using the fingers of the dominant hand, start tapping the side of the opposite hand (the "karate chop" spot), while repeating your setup statement three times. Then, tap each of the following meridian points 5 to 7 times. As you tap, continue to focus on the fear/pain/belief by reciting a brief reminder phrase, such as *"my spouse's illness."*

Top of head: governing vessel

Eyebrow: bladder meridian

Side of the eye: gallbladder meridian

Under the eye: stomach meridian

Under the nose: governing vessel

Chin: central vessel

Collarbone: kidney meridian

Under the arm: spleen meridian

Step Four: *Rate the intensity level.* Once you have completed one round of tapping, rate the intensity level of your fear/pain/belief. Compare it to your baseline. Repeat the sequence as necessary, to continue to reduce the level of intensity.

How it Can Help

Tapping has been shown to assist in the treatment of anxiety, depression, chronic pain, and insomnia. It can also provide relief from emotional disorders, addictions, and the symptoms of PTSD. Because tapping is free and simple to master, anyone can make use of this powerful method of self-healing. Tapping has been shown to provide real, lasting breakthroughs for folks who have had less than desirable outcomes with medication or psychotherapy. While psychotherapy does reduce stress, it doesn't result in immediate, measurable changes within the physical body like tapping can. For example, in one randomized controlled trial, cortisol, a stress hormone, was reduced by an average of twenty-four percent (with some participants experiencing a fifty-percent reduction) after only one hour-long tapping session. In comparison, participants who received an hour's worth of traditional talk therapy received no such benefit. Because of these types of results, many psychotherapists have actually added EFT to their toolbox.

Given how relatively new this modality is, there have already been some dramatic examples of success with EFT documented throughout the world. For over ten years, Dr. Dawson Church, founder of The Stress Project, has been working with war veterans suffering with PTSD and has seen symptoms such as flashbacks and nightmares reduced by over sixty percent after only six EFT sessions. In fact, his program has conducted eight randomized, controlled trials that have successfully demonstrated the safety and efficacy of tapping for PTSD. In a 2013 study, EFT was found to significantly reduce the psychological stress of veterans with PTSD. Even more profound was the fact that not only was their stress reduced, more than half of those participants no longer met the criteria for PTSD! Dr. Church has been so successful in treating veterans that the Veterans Administration now recognizes EFT as a safe, holistic approach to the treatment of PTSD.

Similar success has been realized by The Tapping Solution Foundation (TTSF), established by Nick, Jessica, and Alex Ortner, along with Dr. Lori Leyden, founder of Create Global Healing. TTSF has been providing ongoing trauma services and training to parents, children, health care providers and others in response to the 2012 tragedy at Sandy Hook Elementary School in Newtown, Connecticut. In yet another example, an organization called Project LIGHT Rwanda has been using EFT (along with other strategies) with orphan genocide survivors in Rwanda and has realized phenomenal outcomes. Project LIGHT saw individual trauma symptoms drop as much as thirty-seven percent in one year alone. Indeed, the beauty of the EFT modality is that it is a free gift that can be learned by almost anyone in a matter of minutes, giving folks all over the world access to their innate state of well-being.

Chapter 16 - Crystals and Healing Stones

Crystals, stones, minerals, rocks, gems . . . many of us use those words interchangeably, but is there a difference? Most of what we call crystals are actually minerals or a combination of minerals. Some of those minerals form beautiful crystals, with atoms that organize themselves into one of seven identifiable crystal systems or geometric patterns. Most crystals are formed through natural geologic processes that occur within the earth, requiring a specific environment of heat, space, time, and pressure. In their natural state, crystals simply look like rocks, but once we cut and polish them, they become the gemstones that we know and love.

Amorphous stones, like opal and amber, are non-crystalline; their atoms have solid bonds but don't form the same geometric patterns found in crystals. *Aggregates* form when thousands of microscopic crystals grow together. These stones sometimes look amorphous, but they are crystalline in nature. Agates and jaspers are examples of aggregates.

Although we often think of crystals as being rare, most of the rocks that make up our planet are crystalline, as are certain parts of our human body, most notably our skeleton and tooth enamel. Perhaps our fascination with crystals and our belief in their healing potential is driven by that fact that our very bodies contain these crystalline components.

It is well known that crystals hold special properties, making them ideal for a variety of modern-day technologies, many of which we take for granted. Quartz is arguably the most versatile and widely used crystal. For example, when pressure is applied to quartz, it generates an electric charge, known as the *piezoelectric effect*. This electric charge can be used to ignite gas, which is why quartz is used in many gas-powered appliances, such as grills and ovens. The opposite effect is also true—quartz crystals can receive an electrical charge, process the energy, and then transmit that energetic vibration outward. This property enables quartz to be used in radios, digital watches, and transistors, as well as to power most digital electronic devices. But quartz is not the only crystal with these unique properties. Silicon crystals are used in computers, tablets, cell phones, and televisions, while liquid crystals are used in the display screens. Ruby crystals have the ability to focus energy, and are, therefore, employed in lasers. As you can see, much of what makes crystals technologically beneficial has to do with the energetic vibration (frequency) they emit or produce. Could that mean that the human body is also beneficially impacted by the frequency of crystals?

According to Google, over the past five years, searches related to *crystal healing* have more than doubled. But is there any truth to the theory that crystals and stones hold healing properties? There's no doubt that humans have long been fascinated by them, using gemstones to create beautiful jewelry and protective amulets, as well as for ceremonies and rituals. As a young girl, I learned about birthstones, specific gemstones that correspond to each calendar birth month. Although I wasn't aware at the time, there are also *astrological* gemstones associated with each zodiac sign. Wearing one's birthstone is said to bring good luck and protection. I remember being disappointed that my birthstone was topaz, a golden colored stone that seemed rather boring compared to the more stunning sapphire, diamond, or emerald. As an adult, I now realize that topaz can be found in a variety of colors, but I actually quite like the golden hue. I've since learned that golden, or yellow, topaz is a wonderful stone for manifesting our heart's desire, so I guess I should have been a bit more appreciative that I was born in November.

What are Crystals and Healing Stones?

Since the dawn of time, humans have had an intimate relationship with crystals and stones. Recorded use of talismans and amulets dates back at least 60,000 years (the Upper Paleolithic period), when beads carved from mammoth ivory were found in a Russian grave. Amber amulets and beads have been discovered that date back 30,000 and 10,000 years, respectively. Jewelry made from jet (coal formed from carbonized/fossilized wood) was discovered in Paleolithic graves in Switzerland and Belgium, and there is evidence that malachite was mined in Sinai back in 4000 BC.

Historically, the ways in which these crystals and stones were utilized were numerous. Seeking stones that would provide protection and health, Ancient Egyptians made jewelry and amulets from lapis lazuli, turquoise, carnelian, emerald, and clear quartz. The Egyptians were also known to use stones for cosmetic purposes; ground galena (lead ore) and malachite, for example, were used as eyeshadow. Green stones were used by the Egyptians, as well as the ancient Mexicans during burials, because they represented the heart of the deceased. Ancient Greeks wore amethyst to prevent drunkenness and hangovers and rubbed hematite (iron ore) on their bodies before battle to make themselves invincible. The Ancient Chinese had an affinity for jade and used it to make musical chimes. In both China and South America, jade was considered to be a healing stone for the kidney, and in ancient China and Mexico, it was popular in burial ceremonies; the deceased were often dressed in jade *armor* or masks. Turquoise represented strength and health to the Aztecs and Mayans, while jaspers were associated with strength and calm.

Crystals and gemstones have long played a role in religious history, as well, including Islam, Christianity, Hinduism, and Buddhism. Within the Islamic faith, the fourth Heaven, as written in the Koran, is said to be composed of carbuncle (garnet). Although the Christian church banned amulets in 355 AD, gemstones, particularly sapphires, remained popular with clergy members during the Middle Ages, as they were thought to symbolize Heaven. The Kalpa Tree, sacred to both Hindus and Buddhists, is said to be comprised entirely of precious gemstones, and in the ancient sacred text, the Ratnapariksha of Buddhabhatta, written in the sixth century BC and believed to be Buddhist in origin, gemstones were ranked according to caste.

Between the eleventh and seventeenth centuries, precious and semi-precious stones were revered for their healing properties, many of them being used as a complement to traditional herbal remedies. Although this practice was still accepted during the Enlightenment, the mindset of the time prompted a search for a more scientific explanation behind the practice. Eventually, the use of stones in healing fell out of favor in Europe. Nevertheless, to this day, crystals and stones continue to hold meaning to civilizations throughout the world. For example, even now, jade is thought to bring healing and luck, and turquoise is still considered to be sacred, particularly to Native Americans. A resurgence in the popularity of crystals and healing stones began in earnest in the 1980s. But, as we've seen with other so-called New Age practices, the use of stones for healing has deep historical roots.

How they Work

Because there are no research studies that have demonstrated the medical efficacy of crystals, most scientists attribute positive outcomes to the placebo effect, which they say provides an indirect psychological benefit. Indeed, there is an overwhelming amount of scientific evidence that demonstrates the power of our minds to heal our bodies. In fact, Ted Kaptchuck, Ph.D., director of the Program in Placebo Studies at Harvard Medical School says that these results are not just in our heads. Rather, he says, the placebo effect is a real biological process. When a person engages with the placebo, certain areas of the brain light up, and natural pain suppressors, like endorphins and dopamine, are released. But is that all there is to the *magic* of crystals? Or could there be something deeper at work, an inherent property of the crystals that simply can't be measured with our current technology? Given the plethora of historical anecdotal evidence, we must at least consider the latter. In fact, there are several physics principles that back up the idea that crystals can affect our human body; so to understand the philosophy behind crystal healing, we must first lay some scientific groundwork.

As we learned in part one, everything is energy vibrating at a particular frequency, including crystals, which vibrate at different frequencies depending upon their molecular structure, size, thickness, and color (*light frequency*). We also know that certain systems within our bodies operate by way of tiny electrical currents, which is why your doctor can check the health of your heart with an electrocardiogram. Our nervous and digestive systems also function this way, through electric impulses or the rearrangement of charged particles. The World Health Organization (WHO) has determined that our bodies can actually be influenced by low-frequency electric fields. In fact, according to the WHO, both electric and magnetic fields (EMFs) can generate voltages and currents in the body. Erring on the side of caution, The International Agency for Research on Cancer (IARC), an organization run by the WHO, stated that it is possible that EMFs cause cancer in humans. Scientific building block #1: *Everything in our world operates at a particular frequency, and certain frequencies have the power to impact our human body both positively and negatively.*

Now, because healing stones are often used in conjunction with the chakra system of the body, we need to do a deeper dive into this energetic system that was only briefly touched on in the beginning of part three. The chakras are spinning wheels of invisible energy that line the spine, from the base of the spine to the top of the head (the crown)—where matter meets consciousness. Every organ and system of the body is associated with one of the seven chakras; therefore, if one of our chakras is out of alignment, it may eventually result in a physical symptom. Many mental, emotional, and psychological issues can be addressed through our chakra system as well because they, too, often have an energetic origin.

Each chakra resonates at a specific vibrational frequency and expresses as a particular color. Coincidently, the chakra colors are sequenced exactly like the colors of the rainbow (it's actually not a coincidence, at all . . . it's physics). You see, everything on the electromagnetic spectrum is a type of light, and the human eyeball is only able to register a tiny segment of that spectrum. The chakras, like the rainbow, encompass all of the colors that our human eyes can see. Colors, aka *light frequencies*, arrange themselves in order of wavelength—the longer the wavelength, the lower the frequency and vice versa. Believe it or not, you learned about this in your grade school science class. Remember the mnemonic ROY G BIV? It stands for: Red, Orange, Yellow, Green, Blue, Indigo, and Violet. Red, the color of our 1st chakra, has the longest wavelength (lowest frequency) in the sequence, while Violet, the color of our 7th chakra, has the shortest wavelength (highest frequency). The chart on the next page describes the seven chakras in more detail:

Chakra	Location	Color	Responsibilities
First – Root	base of spine	red	survival, safety
Second – Sacral	lower abdomen	orange	creativity, sexuality
Third– Solar Plexus	naval	yellow	Identity, personal power
Fourth – Heart	center of chest	green	love, compassion
Fifth – Throat	throat	blue	communication, personal truth
Sixth – Third Eye	center forehead	Indigo	insight, intuition
Seventh - Crown	top of the head	violet	enlightenment, wisdom

So what does all of this have to with crystal healing? Well, this is where scientific building block #2 comes in: the physics principle of *entrainment*. Entrainment, or synchronization, is a natural phenomenon that describes the way frequencies, when situated in close proximity and allowed to interact, will adjust, until they all resonate together. The energy of a higher amplitude (higher frequency) will positively influence a similar energy of lower amplitude (lower frequency). Entrainment can be classified as either *mechanical*, when it occurs among non-living objects, or *biological*, when it involves living organisms. An example of mechanical entrainment takes place when two electric clothes dryers are placed close to one another—they will start to oscillate in unison. Biological entrainment can be seen in the synchronized illumination of fireflies.

Entrainment is a fascinating phenomenon that offers a scientific explanation for the way in which crystals can be used for healing; it is believed that the human body will also entrain with a higher amplitude energy source. Compared to our bodies, the crystal will always emit the higher amplitude frequency, because its specific geometric structure makes it much more stable. Even though the human body contains some crystalline components, we are not entirely crystalline; therefore, we will entrain to the higher frequency of the crystal we are working with. For a beginner, one of the easiest ways to utilize crystals and healing stones is to simply choose a stone that matches the color of the chakra you'd like to balance. For example, suppose I were having trouble communicating my needs to my partner (communication issues correspond to the fifth chakra). I could find a piece of lapis lazuli or turquoise—blue stones that are similar in frequency to the fifth chakra—and place it on the base of my throat or wear it somewhere on my body. In this way, the crystal will vibrationally stabilize my fifth chakra, entraining it to the higher frequency of the stone.

There are many ways in which crystals and healing stones can be incorporated into one's life. Not only can crystals be used with the chakra system, each stone has its own set of healing and metaphysical properties and can, therefore, be used individually or in combination with other stones. One way to harness the combined power of crystals is to use them in a grid, which amplifies their energy, helping to focus and expand one's healing intention. Folks who are energetically sensitive often find that they are inexplicably drawn to certain stones and are guided in how to use them effectively. Recently, within the span of one week, two separate friends of mine (who have never met) felt compelled to gift me with a piece of indigo gabbro, commonly called mystical merlinite. Mined in Madagascar, indigo gabbro is a relatively new crystal that is actually a combination of multiple minerals (an aggregate). It is said to be useful in the treatment of swelling, infections, fevers, and immune system disorders. Metaphysically, indigo gabbro helps with the understanding of one's spiritual gifts and natural intuitive abilities. Knowing that there are no coincidences, I look forward to working with this stone, allowing its frequency to nurture my spiritual gifts and abilities.

How they Can Help

Because they are so versatile, abundant, and easily acquired, healing stones can be a wonderful part of a comprehensive, holistic health plan. They can be used to support all sorts of healing processes, whether emotional, mental, spiritual, or physical. Not only are crystals beneficial for healing, they are also helpful for protecting us from potentially harmful energies. As mentioned earlier, humans are constantly bombarded by all sorts of EMFs, simply due to the world in which we live. EMFs are emitted from power lines, microwaves, computers, cellphones and towers, Wi-Fi routers, and more. An overexposure to EMFs can have a detrimental effect on our body; symptoms can include fatigue, joint or muscle pain, insomnia, anxiety or depression, restlessness and irritability, and loss of focus and memory, not to mention their possible carcinogenic effect. Certain stones such as black tourmaline, shungite, and hematite work to shield us from EMFs, keeping energetic imbalances from becoming physical symptoms.

Crystals help us manifest our intentions and remind us of our connection to the Earth. They can best be thought of as one more tool in your holistic toolbox. In the world of physics, the purpose of any tool is to make it easier to accomplish your goal, by expending less energy. So, no matter your objective, crystals and healing stones enable you to easily access the vibrational, healing frequencies that you are seeking.

Chapter 17 - Your Journey Awaits

You have now had the opportunity to explore a number of modalities that have the potential to jump start your journey of awakening—recognizing yourself as so much more than just a physical body. Some of these practices will light you up. They will resonate with your inner *knowingness*; some will not. Think about how you *felt* as you read each chapter. Did you find yourself smiling inside? Did you feel joy? Hope? Peace? Possibility? Did the material seem familiar? If so, it's an indication that you were vibrating in harmony with the information. Start with those practices first. As you learn and grow, you may find that you circle back to some of the other modalities. Engaging with the practices that ring true to you will help you discover your core essence, communicate with that essence, and then embark on a path of health and wholeness. And, if that weren't enough, a natural byproduct of your spiritual awakening will be a stronger connection to God.

Although I had been taking baby steps throughout my life, my own journey of awakening began in earnest after my Reiki I training in 2014. That was when my whole world began to change. Once I let go of the fear, primarily the fear of judgment, I was able to allow the Universe to guide me. The practices in this book are just some of the many modalities I explored, as I uncovered more and more of my authentic self. I stopped listening to what others thought I should do, and I started honoring my own internal guidance system, which led to an enormous amount of freedom and joy—happiness like I had never known! I felt like I had truly been *born again* (to borrow a phrase from my old life). Make no mistake . . . my struggles didn't just vanish into thin air. Human beings come to this earthly playground to *experience* life—its beauty and its sorrow. That being said, once I opened up my connection to Source, to the Divine, things became easier to deal with. Painful lessons took much less time to understand and incorporate; angry episodes were not as frequent or intense; love in all forms was able to express through me in a way that felt so real, so true.

Due to the profound changes that have occurred over the past few years, my life looks nothing like it once did. Letting go of fear and strengthening my connection to Source has enabled me to bask in God's love and then share it with others. Rather than abandoning my faith, I simply enlarged it. Slowly but surely I came to understand that my Christian perspective, the one I had grown up with, wasn't bad, it was simply too small…my view of God too limited. Instead of operating from a place of joy and connection, my faith was rooted in judgment and fear, whether I acknowledged it then or not. The practices in this book allowed me to expand and grow, to include the ideas, principles, and concepts that resonated with my internal know-ingness—those feelings that I had as a teenager but decided to ignore. None of this would have been possible, though, if I had remained inside my comfort zone.

I get it . . . stepping out of our comfort zone can be . . .well, uncomfortable! It takes courage. It requires us to trust in a Divine plan that we can't always see from ground level, *knowing* that the Universe has our back...that it knows what we need when we need it. The Universe also knows what's not in our best interest. Remember that Garth Brooks song, *Unanswered Prayers*? I, too, have often thanked God for not giving me the things I thought I wanted, because I've realized (later) that what God had in mind was so much better. So, as I continue my journey, I listen to those intuitive nudges and follow my passion, engaging with the people and experiences that light me up. When I'm feeling joyful, I know that I'm connected, receiving inspiration, and on the right track. And that is what I desire for you—joy, inspiration, connection. A sense of Divine purpose and fulfillment.

No one but *you* know what lies on your path. For that reason, no one but *you* can decide which way to go, what decision to make, or where meaning will be found. Your family, friends, and church leaders might be very well intentioned, but they have their own paths to discover. Can they provide you with insight and inspiration? Absolutely! But if we continue to live the journey of others—no matter how wonderful those others are—our own gifts will remain hidden. God is waiting for you to say *YES!*

I'm ready. I *am* willing to live a courageous life, to step outside my comfort zone for the chance of a lifetime. The chance to experience the freedom of glorious authenticity. And, as more and more of us learn to live authentically, we give others permission to do the same.

Thank you for sharing in my journey. I'm so happy that our paths have crossed. Remember, there are no coincidences. Perhaps this was a God-instance.

"It really boils down to this: that all life is interrelated. We are all caught in an inescapable network of mutuality, tied into a single garment of destiny. Whatever affects one destiny, affects all indirectly."

Martin Luther King Jr.

Resources: Part Three

Books:

Women's Bodies, Women's Wisdom by Christiane Northrop

Awakening Intuition by Mona Lisa Schultz

Second Sight by Judith Orloff

The Biology of Belief: Unleashing the Power of Consciousness, Matter and Miracles by Bruce Lipton

Websites:

Subtle Energies & Energy Medicine Journal Archives:
http://journals.sfu.ca/seemj/index.php/seemj/index

International Center for Reiki Training (ICRT):
https://www.reiki.org/

Learn more about EFT and veterans:
https://dawsonchurch.com/

Learn more about Create Global Healing and Project LIGHT: https://www.tappingsolutionfoundation.org/

The Tapping Solution Foundation:
https://www.tappingsolutionfoundation.org/

Learn more about crystals and healing stones:
https://hibiscusmooncrystalacademy.com/

Afterward

I met the author of this important book because we both worked in veterans' services in the same state. We lunched together on many a sunny afternoon, talking about our shared passion for health promotion in the military community. Reiki for Vets was her heart work, and my resiliency retreats for veterans was mine. We both believed that healing was possible, and that people could become more resilient by integrating spiritual practices of their choice into their daily routines. Resilience has been most frequently defined as positive adaptation despite adversity, and few theories are more appropriate for working with veterans struggling with reintegration than Resiliency Theory.

Resilience can be trained and taught and is useful for both military trauma survivors and for an average person with absolutely zero trauma history. Frankly, we can all use more of it.

The dialogue surrounding resilience is uniquely appealing to veterans. Studying resilience involves identifying the protective personality traits and behaviors that promote growth and looking for practical ways that programming can strengthen and encourage accessing such traits.

Original research on Resiliency Theory came out of the fields of social work and social psychology, but unlike more problem-oriented theories, it came about after inquiry into characteristics demonstrated by survivors of trauma. Researchers began first by asking the question of why some survivors fared better after difficulty than others who experienced the same events.

Dr. Emmy Werner spent three decades studying children labeled "at-risk." In reality, the stories and backgrounds of these children would break anyone's heart. They came to Werner's social workers from abject poverty and abusive homes. Some had parents suffering with mental illness and were basically orphans. Some actually were orphans without relatives or resources to take them in. She studied over 700 children to look for common traits in the ones who managed to rise above their "at-risk" status. To Dr. Werner, rising above simply meant becoming an independent and functional adult, avoiding law enforcement involvement, institutionalization for mental health problems, substance abuse, etc. Her research found that 36% of those children were thriving and achieving success in school, professions, and relationships. They self-reported high levels of happiness and quality of life. They all had some similar qualities and personality indicators, and Dr. Werner codified these as resilient traits. Kids who tested as socially responsible, adaptable, tolerant, and achievement-oriented seemed to thrive, especially if they also had excellent communication skills and high self-esteem.

Follow-on studies demonstrated important resilient traits in other countries and populations, with marked similarities existing in thriving survivors. Dr. Michael Rutter's work with at-risk children in Britain highlighted the importance of having a relaxed attitude, demonstrating high self-efficacy, and having good social support in cultivating resilience. Self-efficacy is the belief that you can accomplish something, and it predicts performance as well as the ability to connect with others.

Researchers repeatedly found in numbers both practically and statistically significant that the ability to self-correct, demonstrate confidence, and exude sociability helped individuals thrive despite dire circumstances and trauma histories. By 1995, researchers had clearly demonstrated a case for the existence of key, identifiable traits that made a person resilient. The question moving forward became not whether resilience was real, but whether it could be cultivated.

If a person with strong social support spent time on self-regulating their nervous system and took part in spiritual or purposeful practices, could they become more resilient? The answer was an affirmative one. Put simply, people can train themselves to be resilient for those times when hardship comes unexpectedly. Controlled pressure followed by specific exercises to de-escalate the body's reaction creates the ability to handle more pressure next time. Cultivation is core to the theory's concept; the resiliency model was developed to highlight the process whereby an individual moves through stages of biopsy-chospiritual (holistic, whole-person) homeostasis. Simple studies have consistently highlighted the model's central premise, that disruption followed by time and self-care aimed at reintegration actually cultivates resilient traits.

Spiritual or purposeful practice is a key component of resilient trait cultivation. I believe that spiritual practice is mentally healthy, and it is what we are neurologically wired for. From a professional perspective, I believe in the pursuit of spiritual practice because the data tell us that it matters to mental health. I am a health scientist with no training or skills in theology. Though there are a million reasons to cultivate a relationship with your own faith, I invite you to read the work of savvier leaders to talk about those. In my work on spirituality and resilience, I focus particularly on those reasons for belief that show up in our bodies.

Whether speaking from a secular or religious position, the question of divine connection always comes up when one discusses human mental health and happiness. My favorite researcher in the field of social work spent years immersed in interviews with people about happiness, vulnerability, and shame. Dr. Brene Brown's work found that faith mattered a great deal to happy people. Without exception, spirituality – the belief in connection, a power greater than self, and interconnections grounded in love and compassion emerged as a component of resilience.

Social psychologists discuss human needs as happening in hierarchy, with the need for transcendence being the highest. In this secular sense, transcendence is defined as the need to help others seek deep meaning and to discover it for oneself. Our personal spirituality is interwoven with our physical body and our mental and emotional processes.

That is perhaps the great contribution that this book makes—it provides a roadmap for the myriad ways people can practice spirituality, faith, or religion. If such practices make a person resilient, this work is a guide to incorporating them into daily life. If you learned anything from the preceding pages and Dr. Brown's powerful words, I hope you take away that such pursuits are worth the time.

Kate Hendricks Thomas, PhD teaches for George Mason University's Department of Global and Community Health. She is a Marine Corps veteran and the author of several books, including *Brave Strong True: The Modern Warrior's Battle for Balance.*

About the Author

Dr. Allison Brown is an educator, writer, and seeker. Her search for reconciliation between a newfound spirituality and her traditional Christian upbringing led her on an amazing journey of self-discovery. Her passion is to share those lessons and insights with others who are on their own journey of awakening.

Holding a master's degree in counseling psychology and a doctorate in educational leadership, Allison has worked with students from kindergarten through college and beyond. She attained her National Board Certification in 2013 and is currently employed as the director of school counseling at an alternative school for students with behavioral challenges.

Allison is a Reiki Master Teacher and a Quantum Healing Practitioner, utilizing a spiritual hypnosis modality called Beyond Quantum Healing. Allison has been a two-time featured guest on award-winning author, Debra Moffitt's, Unity Online radio program, Divinely Inspired Living. Her work was published in the Fall 2017 issue of the regional quarterly magazine, *Focus on Fabulous*, the December 2018 issue of *Natural Awakenings* magazine, and the February 2019 edition of the online magazine, *Heart and Humanity*. She is also a syndicated contributor to the *Good Men Project* online magazine.

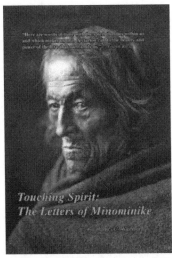

Touching Spirit:
The Letters of Minominike

If you liked this book, you

may like . . .

In the pristine environment of the northern boreal forest, Tulugaq Kagagi muses over a series of letters, written in the vernacular of his grandfather, he recalls his life experiences and the spiritual teachings these events have brought him: transforming his life and worldview.

Through the writing of one man and the inner thoughts of another, we too live through wrenching pain and revitalizing joy and peace. From death to life giving ecstasy, we follow the life journeys of two men separated by generations and culture as they find meaning and rest for their lives.

With the drowning of his parents in 1928, a white infant is orphaned in the Canadian north. Tulugaq Kagagi is lovingly accepted into the home of a childless Ojibwa/Inuit couple, Peepeelee and James. He leaves their home in his teens to continue schooling at seminary in the south. The next thirty years of his life is spent in traditional religious vocation.

During this time, the enfolding of Spirit, its peace and presence slowly fade from his life. In midlife, upon his adoptive father's death, he returns to the cabin of his childhood and discovers a series of letters written by his great-grandfather, Minominike. His religious education and worldview is challenged by the unconditional love and truth expressed in these letters.

As he reads the words of this old man's life his heart is returned to a time of embrace and spiritual oneness that he has not known in decades. Feeling the wind of the Spirit and sensing the inner whisper of a still small voice, meaning and love are again awakened in his heart.

We travel with him on a path of revelation opening his heart to the unity and benevolence surrounding us all. This is a novel that pierces the core of humanity's longing for inner peace and opens for us the simple joy of being.

The letters of Minominike bring insight and encouragement to live in the reality of transcendent love.

https://www.cactusmoonpublishing.com/touching-spirit.html

Made in the USA
Columbia, SC
25 May 2021